The informal gladiolus type.

The proper preparation
of vegetable crops
for exhibit.

Growing for Showing

by Rudy J. Favretti

DOUBLEDAY & COMPANY, INC.
GARDEN CITY, NEW YORK

Contents

Illustration Credits

Introduction

For several years many of my friends have commented on the absence of a little book on the growing and preparation of horticultural material for garden shows. I too have noticed that there is precious little available on the subject. There is quite a bit available on the staging of shows and the production of large-scale exhibits, but so little for the amateur.

Through the encouragement of many, I decided to write such a book. It is intended strictly for the amateur garden hobbyist, specifically garden club members, both men and women, 4–H and FFA members, and the neighborhood groups who like to show what they grow. This book is designed for reading in an evening or two so that it will not take too much time away from gardening. That is why it is so concise and compact. Volumes could be written on the subject but these would be for the professionals, and the various plant societies offer excellent, detailed material for them.

The Federated Garden Club members have their wonderful *Handbook* published by the National Council of State Garden Clubs, Incorporated. This work does not intend to duplicate the handbook, only add to it, especially in Part One on Culture and Part Three which covers grooming and conditioning.

For the nonorganized backyard gardener, this book is intended to provide a source of information on how to grow and select exhibition material which can be entered in the many garden shows held all over the country.

I have not attempted to cover every crop in this book. If I had, it would be voluminous and too awkward and time consuming to read. Instead, I have selected the most popular crops. Those not mentioned, in most cases, are related to the ones discussed here and their growing conditions and selection are similar.

I sincerely hope that the reader has as much fun in reading this book and exhibiting at shows as I have had in writing it and for fourteen years exhibiting and judging at garden shows and fairs. Growing and showing is a lot of fun and every gardener should partake of it.

Before closing, I wish to thank several people who helped in encouraging me to put this in writing: Mr. William Haynes who has been an inspiration in getting started; Mr. Stanley Papanos for doing the line drawings; the folks at the Garden Exchange, in Trumbull, Conn., for encouraging me and loaning me the many half tones used in this book; Mr. Arthur Bobb, Extension Pomologist, and the late Dr. Richard Sudds, professor of Pomology, University of Connecticut, for the advice on the section on fruit; Messrs. Owen Trask, Joseph Lent, and Robert O'Knefski for teaching me how to judge; Mrs. Ronald Macdonald and Mrs. Norman Pierson of the Connecticut Federated Garden Clubs for their comments and suggestions; and last my wonderful wife and family for their help and encouragement.

Storrs, Conn.   R.F.

GROWING FOR SHOWING

1

Why Grow to Show

There isn't a gardener alive whose soul hasn't filled with joy over the mature product of a seed or seedling planted several months earlier. Be this product a glistening flower, a plump vegetable, or a juicy fruit, the satisfaction is the same.

Haven't you experienced this joy? Of course you have and so has every other gardener. After working hand in hand with nature to produce a good flower, vegetable, or fruit you are justified in being proud of your accomplishments.

Garden shows have been developed over the years by gardeners as a place for them to share this joy and exhibit their skills of growing an outstanding horticultural specimen. A show is a place for friendly competition and an exchange of ideas in gardening. It further gives the non-gardening viewers an opportunity to see what a perfect horticultural specimen should look like.

There is no better way to develop an appreciation for plants than to grow them for show purposes. Growing for showing means everyday association with the plants in your garden. You will become more aware of the functions of nutrient elements in plant growth. You will learn the effects of environment upon your plants. You will further learn how to modify this environment to achieve a certain purpose. By practicing the arts of a showman, like disbudding, pinching, and lighting, you will learn how a plant behaves under the hand of man.

After a season or two of growing for showing, you will observe that all varieties do not produce at equal rates nor do they hold up as well in the garden or on the show table. By having a show as a goal to work toward, your sense of variety selection will become highly developed and you will become more critical of what you grow. This is a healthy practice for every gardener to develop in order to help him select good varieties from the many new ones that confront him today. You will no longer want to be bothered with the varieties that tend to produce malformed petals, flecked petals, or those that simply produce weak stems and lack floriferousness. Just as these varieties are not good for the show table, neither are they good specimens for your garden.

You have only to read the newspapers to observe that garden shows are extremely popular with women. Garden club members have been encouraged to exhibit horticultural specimens at shows for many years and most clubs even conduct shows of their own. The trend today indicates that garden shows conducted by neighborhood communities are becoming increasingly popular. Exhibiting at these shows provides an excellent recreational need for a segment of the population just as a golf tournament does for another segment.

Men, through the men's garden clubs and local fairs, have found the growing and exhibiting of show specimens to be an intriguing pastime. Many men who garden as a hobby have discovered that it is fascinating to carry their hobby a step further into the mechanical techniques of staking and disbudding, as well as the other practices associated with the growing of a show product (Photographs 1 and 2).

There are few better ways to teach children plant behavior, responsibility, and good sportsmanship than to encourage them to grow and exhibit show specimens. I vividly remember the first year that I exhibited at the New London County 4-H Club

Fair. Being an enthusiastic and energetic child, my object was to show as many exhibits of flowers and vegetables as possible. I therefore hastily collected all I could exhibit, without first reading the show list and instructions on exhibiting, and took everything to the fair.

The exhibits remained in place overnight and were judged the next morning. That night I hardly slept in anticipation of the judging. But the results were very disappointing. I received one blue award, a few reds and many whites. I also had about as many specimens that received no award at all. My decision at that point was that I had been too anxious to build up a collection of ribbons without even considering how a ribbon is won and that actually, after all is said and done, the ribbon is not the important thing.

A quick inspection of the other exhibits revealed that it wasn't the largest beet that received the first award. I further learned that when the show schedule calls for five specimens of zinnias it means this and that an extra bloom or two thrown in to make up for the inferiority of the others means no award. I learned to follow directions. I further learned to exhibit only the best produce that I had. I learned to be a good sport. And was I ever ashamed to discover that greediness does not pay!

My wonderful parents had been trying to instill these principles in me over the years with some degree of success and the 4-H fair climaxed their teachings and made a great impression so that at future fairs and shows, and I hope in everyday life, these principles remained lasting.

Besides teaching you and your children plant behavior, increasing your appreciation of plants, and highly developing your gardening skills, growing show material is a relaxing hobby. Growing for showing requires little more time than regular gardening, so while you are devoting this time to your garden you will be forced to forget the many problems that this busy twentieth-century world bring us.

PART ONE

Culture

2

The Soil

In "A Land of Plenty," Jerrold states of the earth, "Just tickle her with a hoe and she laughs with a harvest." Immediately this reminds us that our soil is truly a wonderful thing. But at the same time we must realize that in spite of its wonder the soil needs some other things along with the "tickle."

Soils have many basic functions. The first and most apparent is to hold the plant upright by anchoring its roots. Secondly, a soil must hold moisture without becoming waterlogged if good plant growth is expected. We usually say that soils having this property are well drained. At the same time the soil must be loose enough to allow for the free passage of oxygen through it. Lastly, the soil most hold nutrients in ready availability to the plants. We can no more expect to grow good show specimens without the proper nutrients than we can to grow a healthy child on an unbalanced diet.

BUILDING UP THE SOIL

In preparing the show garden, our first consideration must be the condition of the soil. Sandy soils do not hold enough water and nutrients in ready availability to the plants. Furthermore, sandy soils, because of their large spaces between the particles, allow all of the water, practically speaking, to leach through. Clay soils, on the contrary, retain moisture and nutrients but, because of their composition, compact so severely that proper aeration is impaired. Dwarfed, stunted plants result from this condition. The showman cannot afford to grow his specimens in either of these extremes.

The ideal soil is one that contains sand as the basic ingredient with particles of clay dispersed throughout. Clay particles serve as tiny "magnets" to hold the nutrient elements in place and in ready availability to the plants. Scientifically these particles are known as soil colloids. The ideal soil must also contain organic matter such as manure, compost, peat moss, or leafmold in enough quantity to make the soil friable and loose in texture. Organic matter in the soil helps to improve the aeration, acts as a "sponge" to hold water, and further improves the colloidal content of the soil. Upon breaking down, therefore, it releases nutrients to the soil and the plants in it.

Let us hope that you are fortunate enough to have a soil in your garden that answers the above description in its basic make-up, realizing that practically all soils have to have organic matter added from time to time. Most of us, however, are not that fortunate and have to expend time and energy improving the soil in the show garden. Even though it involves a lot of work, this "soil building" process cannot be overstressed if we expect good exhibition specimens. We can no more expect to grow "winners" in an inadequate soil than we can build a sturdy strong house on a weak, unstable foundation.

Most soils are not so bad that we have to completely remove the poor soil and replace it with a good soil mixture, although sometimes this is the case. In my own garden that basic ingredient was clay with a little sand present. I, therefore, had to add a little more sand and plenty of organic matter. This was accomplished by digging a trench eighteen inches deep, two feet long, and the width of the garden, which in this case was three feet (Fig. 1). Then I spread an inch of sand

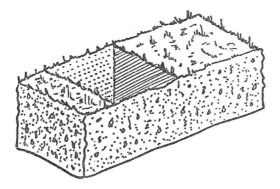

Fig. 1. This drawing shows a trench dug at one end of the garden to absorb the extra volume of soil mixture to be created by the incorporation of organic matter into the soil for soil improvement.

and four to five inches of organic matter over the surface of the entire bed. (I used a mixture of peat moss and well-rotted manure.) In spading the organic matter and sand into the soil, I began at the end of the bed where I had previously dug the trench. The extra volume, made by adding organic matter and sand, was absorbed in the trench where I had removed the soil. Had I not done this, this extra volume would have raised my beds too high after spading. The poor soil from the trench was added to the compost pile and someday it too will be good soil.

The task of improving the soil texture can be backbreaking and involved, but it is necessary for the production of top-notch show specimens. First of all, let's hope that your soil is all right to begin with; and if it isn't, let's hope that you have a vegetable garden where you have gradually built up the soil over the years from which you can "steal" a little piece for your show garden. If you cannot do either of these, then I guess the only solution is to "build up."

THE NUTRIENTS

So far we have talked only about building up the texture of the soil so that it will work efficiently for our plants. Now that our machinery is in order, let us discuss the items we need to add to the soil for proper plant growth.

So far as we know, there are fifteen elements essential to the proper growth of plants and this group is broken into two categories—the major elements and the minor elements. These words "major" and "minor" do not denote importance but rather the amounts in which they are needed by the plant.

The members of the major group are carbon (C), hydrogen (H), oxygen (O), nitrogen (N), phosphorous (P), potassium (K), calcium (Ca), magnesium (Mg), sulphur (S), and iron (Fe). Of these, carbon, hydrogen, and oxygen are not applied by the gardener. They are provided to the plant naturally through the soil, water, and air.

Of the remaining seven elements in the major group, nitrogen, phosphorous, and potassium are called the "big three." These are the elements with which we are most concerned as gardeners, although we must not think for one minute that the rest are not important. N, P, and K are to the plant what bread, meat, milk, and vegetables are to the human being. Calcium is of everyday importance to the gardener too, but it is usually applied to the soil in the form of limestone rather than in a complete fertilizer.

Boron (Bo), copper (Cu), zinc (Zn), manganese (Mn), and molybdenum (Mo) are the minor elements. Like iron in the major group, they are usually present in the soil and are released to the plants if the soil is managed properly. Most of the present-day fertilizers contain traces of some or all of these elements.

THE FUNCTIONS OF THE ELEMENTS IN THE PLANT

As garden showmen we need to concern ourselves with the functions of these elements in the plant. You will find that the terms "cultural perfection," "condition," and "substance" are important ones on the judge's score card. In part, all of these term cover the matter of having the bloom, stem, foliage, or fruit of a specimen in perfect health and condition. Naturally the fifteen elements play an important role in seeing that the specimen you exhibit is culturally perfect.

Let us discuss the roles of the major elements in the next few paragraphs since they are the ones that are most often lacking. As mentioned previously, the minor group is not so likely to be lacking if the soil is managed properly.

Nitrogen   This element is a critical one to the garden showman since it is basically responsible for the production of leaves and stems. A deficiency will produce yellowed (chorotic) foliage and stunted plants. Usually the leaves begin to yellow first on the basal portion of the plant and the yellowing then continues upward toward the tip. Too much nitrogen produces dark foliage and weak, spindly stems. Also, it interferes with flower production, since it hinders the production of carbohydrates which are so important to strong growth and flowering and the eventual life of the specimen on the show table. The weak succulent growth produced by overfeeding with nitrogen is more susceptible to diseases than normal growth. Therefore, it is exceedingly important to maintain a proper balance of nitrogen in the show garden soil.

Nitrogen is very unstable in the soil because of its high solubility in water. During wet seasons, nitrogen is leached from the soil and this means one thing to the showman—watch your plants carefully for nitrogen deficiency.

Phosphorous   Phosphorous stimulates the production of flowers, fruits, and seeds. We needn't say too much more, then, of its importance to the garden showman since most of the material which he exhibits consists of either flowers, fruits, or seeds. With this function in mind, most garden showmen apply a side dressing of superphosphate to their plants a few weeks before they come into flower and thoroughly work it into the soil.

Phosphorous, unlike nitrogen, moves very slowly in the soil; therefore if a side dressing is used, it must be worked into the soil just under the outer leaves of the plant to which it is applied. The feeding roots are in this area. Failure to do this will render the superphosphate useless to the plant for which it was intended for that season's flowering.

Although phosphorous has other important roles in plant growth, those mentioned are the ones that should concern us as showmen. Plants deficient in this element are likely to be dwarfed with dark green foliage and as the deficiency worsens, they may take on a reddish cast. Phosphorous is less likely to become deficient in the soil than nitrogen.

Potassium   Potassium has many functions within the plant. Of these, its importance to cell division and the synthesis of protein and its aid to the movement of carbohydrates within the plant are most important to us.

Plants deficient in potassium are often stunted and will eventually bear chlorotic leaves that, in most cases, dry out along the margins, giving a scorched appearance to the leaves. Chlorosis in the case of potassium deficiency is likely to be more "spotty" than in the case of nitrogen deficiency. Too, potassium deficiency is not usually so severe as nitrogen deficiency in most of our soils.

Calcium   In most parts of the country, calcium is applied to the soil in the form of calcium carbonate, or lime. Calcium has a complicated role in plant growth but basically it is important to the metabolic processes of the plant. In the production of proteins, the plant releases toxic organic acids which calcium helps to neutralize. Without this important role of calcium, these acids would be harmful to the plant.

Magnesium Like the other elements mentioned, this element has many roles in plant growth. To us its most important role is the production of chlorophyll. Without magnesium the proper production of chlorophyll would be impaired and the result would be chlorotic plants that would not function efficiently even if all other growing conditions were ideal.

Sulphur At the expense of being too elementary, it is best to say that sulphur is the element that gives the strong flavor to onions, radishes, cauliflower, cabbage, and their other strong flavored friends. Evidently sulphur has an important role in the production of chlorophyll because when it is absent a condition much like that of nitrogen deficiency exists. The deficiency of sulphur in the soil is rare, compared to the deficiency of the other major elements.

Iron Contrasted to the other major elements discussed, iron is required by the plant in comparatively small amounts. In this respect it is much like the minor elements. Iron deficiency is quite common in certain plants however, especially in those that require acid soil conditions and don't get them.

Although iron is not found in chlorophyll, it is important as a catalyst in its production. Iron chlorosis is quite different from nitrogen chlorosis; instead of being a universal yellowing of the leaf, it appears as a yellowing between the veins of the leaf. As the condition becomes worse these interveinal areas become a bleached-out white. The initial interveinal yellowing often appears as yellow dots, giving the leaf a mottled appearance.

A deficiency of iron in plants can exist even when iron is present in the soil, since certain compounds can combine with iron to render it insoluble for plant use. This condition often occurs in soils that are not acid enough for the plant in question or, as Dr. Curtis Keyes pointed out about twenty years ago, in the case of gardenias, when temperature conditions in the soil are too cool for the proper absorption of iron.

When iron chlorosis exists, the soil pH must be corrected to satisfy the plant by making iron available. This is the most permanent cure, but chelated iron can be used as a temporary adjustment. Simply, chelated iron is iron in a form that can easily and quickly be absorbed by the plant.

THE APPLICATION OF NUTRIENTS

You can see from this discussion how important it is to the exhibitor to provide his plants with the proper elements. Fortunately the fertilizer manufacturers have made the application of these elements easy for us. The major elements need not be applied one by one, which would certainly be a time-consuming task.

The term "complete fertilizer" is a byword to the plantsman. Complete fertilizers contain nitrogen, phosphorous, and potassium. We can purchase a complete fertilizer in many balances: 5–10–10, 5–10–5, 5–8–7, 7–7–7, 10–10–10, and many more. These numbers tell us the percentage of nitrogen, phosphorous and potassium in the fertilizer bag. Nitrogen is always listed first, phosphorous second, and potassium third. Therefore, a 5–10–10 fertilizer contains five per cent nitrogen, ten per cent phosphorous, and ten per cent potassium. This is the ratio used most often by garden showmen since it contains an adequate balance of the "big three." Actually, since nitrogen is "here today and gone tomorrow" in the soil, a 5–10–10 fertilizer should be supplemented with nitrogen in the form of nitrate of soda to raise its amount. In fact, some additional nitrogen might have to be applied from time to time between applications of a complete fertilizer, depending upon how the plant looks.

Fertilizer should be applied to the soil on the basis of soil test recommendations. Most land-grant colleges and experiment stations offer soil testing services either at a slight fee or free of charge. It behooves you as a showman to have your soil tested as a guide for the application of fertilizer or lime.

In most cases the recommendations will suggest the application of a complete fertilizer at a rate that will correct the improper balance of nutrients in the soil. It is wise to have the soil tested at planting time and again five to six weeks before you intend to harvest for exhibition. With long-term crops like tomatoes or mums a third test halfway between those mentioned would be helpful. In normal gardening procedures, soils are tested only once in every two to three years.

Usually your fertilizer schedule will call for three to four pounds of a complete fertilizer at the time of planting, or when growth begins with perennials, for one hundred square feet of soil area. Then a second application should be applied in late June or early July at the same rate. Never should fertilizer be applied within two months of the average date of the first frost, with perennials or shrubs, since these late applications can force new, tender growth.

Sometimes when only nitrogen is lacking, one half to one pound of nitrate of soda can be applied for one hundred square feet of soil area. When only phosphorous is low, superphosphate can be added. However, this method of applying single elements is costly. It is easier and less expensive to apply a complete fertilizer whenever possible.

Fertilizer must never be spaded into the soil. Apply it to the surface of the soil after plowing or spading and rake or cultivate it into the upper two inches. This is where the roots will need it. If spaded in, much of the fertilizer will be too deep for the young plant roots.

You will notice that the complete fertilizers discussed were of the inorganic type. Organics such as cottonseed meal, castor pomace, bone meal, and others are perfectly all right to use as specifics. In fact they are longer lasting in the soil. However, if you intend to use organics you must remember a few basic points.

Organics are slow to take action after application. In fact

when the soil temperatures are below 55 degrees they do not release nutrients to speak of. During warm seasons, however, they can be extremely helpful since their effect is longer lasting than that of inorganics. They are more expensive than inorganic fertilizers, but as some gardeners point out they need not be applied as often during the summer. Suitable grades are 10–6–4 and 10–5–5. They are high enough in nitrogen so that during normal seasons, nitrate of soda is not necessary. It is important, however, to follow soil test recommendations even in this case.

If a particular element is lacking in your show garden soil and the conditions must be corrected fast, it is better to rely on chemical fertilizers. The liquid forms are even faster than the powdered or pelleted types. Liquid fertilizers are a Godsend if a deficiency occurs since it must be corrected immediately to prevent a delay in the plant's growth. Since liquid fertilizers are extremely soluble they have little lasting effect on the soil but they are good "shot-in-the-arm" cures. It is better to apply nonliquid, inorganic fertilizers to the show garden according to the schedule mentioned previously than to use highly soluble types. In other words, we are deciding upon a point part way between liquids and organics as a general practice and in length of effectiveness.

SOIL pH

After all is said and done, we can apply the right fertilizers to our plants at the proper time and at the proper rate, but unless the pH is just right for the plants grown the nutrients will not become available to the plants at the proper level. Maintaining the proper pH is also important to the proper workings of the soil bacteria which are so important in the breaking down of organic matter and the subsequent release of nutrients.

What is pH? Simply, it is the soil reaction measured in units, which is a convenient way of expressing a rather involved chemical relationship of the concentration of hydrogen ions in the soil solution. The *p*H scale runs from zero to fourteen and seven is the neutral point. Soils above *p*H seven are alkaline or "sweet" and below *p*H seven they are acid or "sour" (Figure 2). Most of the plants that we grow prefer a *p*H level between

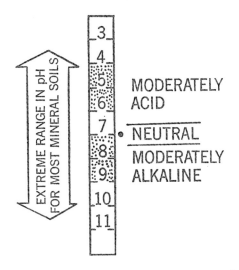

Fig. 2. The *p*H scale.

5.5 and 7.0, but there are those like azaleas, rhododendrons, and mountain laurel that require a lower *p*H (4.5–5.5).

We can realize from Figure 3 that the availability of nutrients varies with the *p*H level and the importance of maintaining the proper level for the plants we grow. In some areas of the country the problem of maintaining the right level is one of acidifying the soil, while in other areas, such as in New England, the problem is one of sweetening the soil through the addition of ground agricultural limestone. Here our soils tend naturally to be acid.

Whichever your situation may be, you can realize by now how the matters of fertilization and maintaining the proper

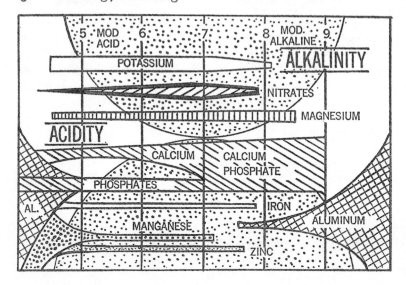

Fig. 3. The availability of nutrients of various pH levels.

pH are interrelated if good show specimens are the object. If possible we should prevent nutrient deficiencies from occurring in the show garden since a deficiency hampers the growth and flowering of our plants. Therefore, proper fertilizer (nutrient) and pH levels must be maintained and this means periodic soil tests.

IRON CHLOROSIS

We have already mentioned iron chlorosis in a general way. However, since it is such a classical example of how the pH of a soil affects the availability of nutrients, it is worth while to discuss it again.

Iron is usually present in soils, especially those high in organic matter. At high pH levels, it becomes bound and unavailable, resulting in a deficiency with interveinal chlorosis.

To correct the problem, the gardener must lower the pH level by applying sulphur or aluminum sulphate according to soil test recommendations. Since the lowering of pH is not a quick process, iron can be applied to the plant or the soil in a chelated form (readily available) to quickly restore this element in the plant. Fortunately iron chelates are being sold today at garden centers so that they are not difficult to obtain. Iron in a non-chelated state is not quickly available to the plant, so the garden showman who has iron deficiency in his plants and refuses to use chelates may not be able to bring his plants back to good health before the show.

ADJUSTING THE SOIL pH

Soil test recommendations will tell you how much lime to apply to sweeten your soil or how much sulphur or sulphates to apply to acidify it. It is best to follow these recommendations carefully. As a general rule, however, to raise the pH one whole unit you will need to apply four to five pounds of ground agricultural limestone, and to raise it two units the application will be ten pounds per 100 square feet. For example, if you have to raise the pH level from 4.0 to 6.0, ten pounds of lime will be required, while only five pounds will raise the level from 4.0 to 5.0.

Unlike fertilizer, lime should be spaded into the show bed at the time of preparation since, if it is applied only to the surface, it will take quite a long time for it to work its way down into the root region. Results are quicker when lime is spaded into the soil.

If you have selected a new area for your show garden where the soil pH has to be drastically readjusted, you would be wise for the first year to grow some crop other than your show specimens until you are sure the pH has risen or lowered to the proper level.

HOW TO TAKE A SOIL SAMPLE

We have referred many times to the importance of adjusting the nutrient and *p*H levels on the basis of soil tests. The results of these tests are only as good as the sampling techniques used. Just going out into the garden and removing a trowelful of soil and then sending it to the lab for testing will not give you the type of test you really want since this sample does not accurately represent the total garden area.

The proper sampling technique is easy but more involved than that just mentioned. First of all, obtain a pail or some other large receptacle and also a trowel. The pail will be used to collect the samples and the trowel is your sampling tool. At one corner of the garden dig a hole, the depth of the trowel, and discard the soil. Then with the trowel, cut a slice along the side of this hole. The central portion of this slice (about two to three inches below ground level) is the critical sample, so you can throw away the soil above and below. Put the sample in the pail (Fig. 4).

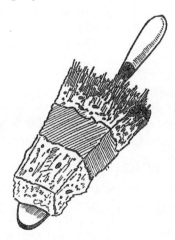

Fig. 4. This is a slice of soil of which the central portion is to be a part of the conglomerate sample.

The job is not yet completed. Now you must repeat this operation in the other three corners of the garden and again in two or three places scattered over the center. After you have collected anywhere from five to ten samples in the pail, shake all of them thoroughly and even use the trowel as a mixer. The result from all this collecting and mixing is a conglomerate sample and if you remove only a cupful of soil from this conglomerate and send it to the laboratory you have sent in an accurate sampling of your show garden. Therefore, the recommendations will be accurate too.

If there is a corner of your garden that does not produce good plants take several samples from this area and make a conglomerate; then send a cupful of this soil to the lab in a separate box or container. This will be tested and the results will be for the problem area only.

The poor practice of not making a conglomerate sample but just sending to the laboratory a trowelful of soil from the garden has resulted in almost fantastic results for some gardeners. I have seen samples of this type where the gardener, by chance, removed the sample from an area where a compost or manure pile had stood the previous year. Therefore, since this was his sample the results were way out of line for the rest of the garden.

One more item before leaving the matter of sampling for soil tests. Be very sure to mark on a piece of paper accompanying the sample your code letter for the sample if you send in more than one. List the past treatments for the garden area from which the sample was taken. For example, list the crops grown there in past years and what fertilizer and lime applications you made. Also list what you intend to grow in the future and any special problems you want answered concerning the soil. These statements will help the person who makes the recommendations for you to be as accurate as possible. This is much like the doctor wanting to know your past health history before diagnosing your present problem.

SOIL FOR HOUSE PLANTS AND FERTILIZATION

House plant soil must be built up too. In fact, it is extremely critical to have the right soil in this case since we are dealing in such a small amount as compared to the garden.

Regular garden loam used by itself for the potting of house plants is not desirable. We therefore need to make a mixture that will provide for proper drainage, moisture-holding capacity, and aeration.

A good soil mixture consists of two parts of good garden loam, two parts of peat moss or compost, and one part of sand. Of course this mixture will vary or need to be varied as to the type of garden loam you have in your area. For example, in Connecticut we prefer three parts of loam rather than two.

Here again, after the mixture is made, the soil *p*H and the nutrients should be adjusted on the basis of soil test recommendations. Soil tests should be made from time to time even on the culture of house plants. In this case knock the plant and soil ball out of the pot and remove a spoonful of soil halfway down the ball. Then place the plant and ball back into the pot. Do this with all of your plants of one kind and make a conglomerate from which you take one sample for the laboratory. This is not difficult for the showman to do since for show purposes he should be growing several pots of one kind or variety of house plants.

Soil tests in the case of potted plants give us another dividend. The accumulation of salts in the soil can build up to a point harmful to the plant roots. A soil test will yield the level of soluble salts and the recommendations may suggest a repotting or a "flushing" of the soil (heavy, thorough watering) to eliminate the salt condition. Adequate, thorough watering as a general practice will usually keep the salts down, however.

Constant feeding of house plants is recommended today rather than heavy monthly feedings. By constant feeding we mean applying small amounts of a weak solution of fertilizer at weekly intervals. Fertilizers approaching a 1–1–3 ratio are suggested. However, you may not be able to find one whose ratio is exactly 1–1–3. For example, one of our popular fertilizers for constant feeding has a 7–6–19 grade. This is not exactly 1–1–3 but it comes close to it. By using constant feeding, we have better control of our house plant soils and by fertilizing according to soil tests and the appearance of the plant we should be able to avoid many of the problems encountered in the old monthly feeding approach.

SOIL WATER

A person who has advanced to the point of growing plants for show purposes need not be reminded of the importance of water in the growth of plants. However, it should be said here that if water is scarce in the show garden we cannot expect to grow award-winning plants.

First of all, we need water to carry those fertilizer elements that we have been discussing into solution so that the plant roots can properly absorb them. Fertilizer applied to dry soil will not help our plants very much.

Water is also needed within the plants to carry manufactured foods as well as fertilizer elements to where they are needed for proper plant functioning. And, furthermore, we shouldn't lose sight of the fact that water is essential in the production of these foods to begin with.

In 1941 a man by the name of Reger did a piece of research on the relation of moisture to the time of bloom of calendulas and larkspurs. The results showed that calendulas started in moist soil and then transferred to dry soil flowered seven days later than those left in the moist soil. He further determined that larkspurs grown in dry soil were delayed eighteen days in flowering.

Dr. Richard Stinson, now on the faculty at Michigan State University, found that African violets flowered earlier, had larger plant diameters, and produced more flowers when they were grown at a constant moisture level than when they were hose watered.

In some of my own experimentation, the results showed that gloxinias are delayed in flowering for as much as two to four weeks when run dry.

A possible explanation for the delay in flowering at low moisture levels is that the photosynthetic rate of the plant is slowed down at these levels. This, therefore, points to the importance of maintaining moist soil in the show garden since the reaction to moisture levels is probably similar in most of the plants we grow for show purposes.

Soils that are properly prepared will hold water to be used by the plants, but this is only a relative thing. When water is taken from the soil either by the plants or through evaporation, even the best soils will be lacking in water. The showman must check his soil regularly to make sure that his soil moisture level is adequate. This can easily be done by digging a hole with a trowel two to three inches deep and feeling of the soil in the bottom of the hole. If the soil is dry, and if nature does not promise to oblige, then water should be applied artificially.

In the show garden, do not apply water by means of sprinklers, especially if you are watering after three o'clock in the afternoon. Avoid wetting the foliage of show plants since wet leaves, warm temperatures, and darkness favor disease invasion. For this reason, the soaker-type hoses are ideal since water runs directly from the hose into the soil without wetting the plants.

It is better not to water at all than to give the soil a light sprinkling. This just teases the plant into producing roots near the soil surface where they can get this water. When the water obtained from these light sprinklings dries out, the roots die and after the next light sprinkling more roots are produced. Therefore, our plants concentrate on making new roots instead of prize blooms or fruits.

When you water the show garden, let the soil soak to a

four- to five-inch depth before changing the hose to another spot in the garden. All environmental factors are critical in the production of good plants, but water is so very important in the production of large-sized plants and flowers.

MULCHING

Of all the garden chores that we as showmen must perform, I think that mulching gives us the most dividends for the time and expense involved. Mulching has four major functions in the show garden.

First of all, a three- to four-inch mulch can keep a lot of water from evaporating away from our soils. This in itself is beneficial since we have shown how critical soil moisture levels are in the production of show specimens. By cutting down the evaporation rate of water, mulching saves watering time and dollars and cents on the water bill. We must still check on the moisture content of the soil even when a mulch is used, but watering time and labor will be greatly reduced.

Another advantage of mulching is that it helps in keeping weeds down. Weeds that grow in the garden only compete for water and nutrients and harbor pests as well. Granted that a few weeds will come through a mulch, the number is greatly reduced and those that are present are so few that they can be removed on our daily inspection walks through the show garden.

At the end of the gardening season, mulches can and should be incorporated into the soil to replenish the organic matter supply. Some mulches add more to the soil in the way of organic matter than others. Buckwheat hulls, one of the neatest and most attractive mulches we have, do not really add great quantities of organic matter although they are very effective in controlling weeds and cutting down on evaporation. Peat moss and sugar cane, on the other hand, may not be as attractive but they do increase the organic matter supply to a greater degree.

To the showman, the fourth benefit of a mulch is invaluable. Mulches, because they absorb rain drops, cut down on the amount of soil spattered onto the foliage stems and flowers of our plants. A judge will eliminate many points from the score card if soil is present on the leaves or the foliage is injured by soil spatter. Yes, soil can be washed off but if there is less to be removed through washing, the risk of damaging the leaves is much less. In the case of soil spattering of petunias, for example, soil spattering on the flower itself leaves a permanent blemish that cannot be removed. Consequently, the flower is ruined as far as exhibiting is concerned.

There are many mulches that can be used. Buckwheat hulls, peat moss, and sugar cane (sold for poultry litter) are the most attractive ones. Straw, weed-free hay, grass clippings, salt marsh hay, and sawdust are less attractive but make good mulches too, and involve less expense than the others. However, they are a little harder to apply.

When sawdust is used, apply one-half to one pound of either nitrate of soda or ammonium nitrate per one hundred square feet of soil area before applying the mulch. This is done to provide enough nitrogen for the plants as well as the bacteria that break down the sawdust. If we neglect doing this, nitrogen deficiency will occur very rapidly.

We can all agree, then, that mulching is a must for all show gardens. The showman who fails to mulch only increases his chances for failure when his specimens ultimately reach the show table.

3

Light

After a whole chapter on the subject the importance of adequate soil conditions is apparent. In the second paragraph of the last chapter we stated: "We can no more expect to grow good show specimens without the proper nutrients than we can grow a healthy child on an unbalanced diet." At this point we might modify the statement to read: "We can no more expect to grow good show specimens without the proper nutrients and *light* . . ." And as we progress we will add the word "temperature" to this list as it too dovetails into the total environmental picture related to plant growth. In other words, no single factor can do the whole job. When one is lacking growth is impaired.

Our discussion of light in this chapter will be divided into two categories—light intensity and light duration.

LIGHT INTENSITY

Light is important for photosynthesis in plants since it provides the energy that converts water and carbon dioxide into carbohydrates (as well as other organic compounds) and oxygen. In general, the higher the light intensity and the greater the photosynthetic rate and the stronger the plant, the greater the number of flowers and size, and the brighter the color. Consequently, in most cases, we as showmen must provide our plants with high light intensities so that photosynthesis may go on at a fast rate.

We must realize, however, that no general rule applies across the board when we deal with living things. First of all, temperature plays an important role in the photosynthetic process. This is a chemical process and as in most chemical reactions the higher the temperature, the faster the reaction. Therefore, with an increase in temperature the photosynthetic rate is also increased. Water, too, contributes to proper photosynthetic action and if it is limited the process is impaired. So you see, basically, how the "law of limiting factors" works in plant growth.

Although our general rule of having as high a light intensity as possible is true in most cases, it does not hold true with some plants. For example, African violets, violets, primroses, and ferns belong to a group of plants that are able to carry on photosynthesis in very low light intensities. Dr. Richard Stinson in his work with African violets showed that the point where they grow and initiate flower buds best is one thousand foot-candle of light. When we consider that on a normal sunny day in the summer in Connecticut the light intensity is between ten thousand to twelve thousand foot-candles, it is apparent that African violets do not require much light to flower. High light intensities, above thirteen hundred foot-candles, will prevent African violets from producing flowers. When the intensity of light falls below three hundred foot-candles, no flowers are formed either.

We conclude, then, that although we must provide our plants with as much light as possible, generally speaking, there are those plants that just won't tolerate it since the high intensities bring about a reduction in chlorophyll in some cases, while in others they cause too high a loss of water owing to the high temperatures associated with high light intensities. These related high temperatures can also cause the fading of flower color which means that in extremely high light intensity areas, such as the Southwest, cheesecloth or lath shade must be provided if the flowers are to be kept from fading.

PHOTOTROPISM

Plants have the habit of bending toward the light and plantsmen call this act "phototropism." Researchers suggest that plants do this because cells elongate more on the side away from the light and thus cause the plant to bend toward the light. Light supposedly destroys the hormone that produces this elongation; that is the reason the cells on the lighted side do not elongate at the same rate as those on the side away from the light.

Phototropism should concern the garden showman. An exhibition plant that bends to one side has many points eliminated from its score. If we turn potted plants from a quarter to a half turn each day, this bending is not visible.

Phototropism occurs out of doors too. This is why experienced gardeners always tell us to locate our gardens so that the plants in them can be viewed from the south side since the flowers themselves will be facing south toward the light. We have a garden at our house that could not be placed according to the above recommendation. Therefore, as I sit at the breakfast table and look out upon the garden I see mostly the backs of the flower heads.

There is little we can do to prevent the occurrence of phototropism in the out-door garden. In the show garden, we have to stake the stems of the flowers so that they will grow straight. Flowers such as lupines, gladioli, and snapdragons will respond to light even after they are picked. It is a good practice to cover the flower heads of all flowers as they are being carried to the show, but especially with these flowers the tissue covering also prevents phototropism.

LIGHT DURATION—PHOTOPERIOD

The length of day is a critical matter for flower bud initiation, flower bud development, and vegetative growth in many plants. To the horticulturist, the chrysanthemum is a classical example of a plant that responds to daylength treatments. Technically this plant will not initiate flower buds unless the day is 14.5 hours in length and will not develop these buds unless the days are 13.5 hours long. Hence, we call the chrysanthemum a "short-day plant."*

When the daylength is longer than 14.5 hours, the chrysanthemum produces only vegetative growth and will not flower. This can easily be illustrated by the chrysanthemums in our own gardens which flower only in the fall when the days are shorter.

Again we cannot discuss one environmental factor without involving another since temperature is critical in flower bud initiation too. Certain plants require definite temperatures for flower by initiation, development, and vegetative growth. Generally speaking, the chrysanthemum requires 60-degree night temperatures for bud initiation. Some varieties, however, prefer slightly higher temperatures and others slightly lower temperatures.

It appears that today we have varieties of garden chrysanthemums that are more particular as to temperature than daylength. This may account for the fact that some varieties flower early in the summer.

Garner and Allard, two United States Department of Agriculture researchers, did much concrete work on photoperiodism using tobacco as their experiment plant. They classed plants into three categories as far as photoperiodic responses are concerned: long-day plants, short-day plants, and indifferent plants or those that flower regardless of daylength.

---

* Actually it is the length of the dark period that is the critical factor, but it is usually easier to make reference to photoperiod in term of daylight rather than darkness.

Photoperiodism is important to the gardener since he should know what triggers the flowering of certain plants. To the garden showman it is extremely important, for he can manipulate the daylength to cause a delay or an advance in the flowering date of certain plants to meet a particular show date.

The length of day is not the same all over the country on a given date. As we move from the south to the north there is a greater difference in the length of day between summer and winter. For example, in New Orleans on the Fourth of July the day is fifteen hours long, while on Christmas Day it is eleven hours long. This is only a difference of four hours between, roughly speaking, the longest and the shortest days. Now let's take Anchorage, Alaska. Here the day is twenty two hours long on July Fourth and slightly under eight hours long on Christmas Day, a difference of fourteen hours. These figures were taken from page 71 of *Florist Crop Production and Marketing* by Dr. Kenneth Post.

Also on page 71 Dr. Post presented a very interesting chart from which the material in Table One was taken. This table simply tells us what approximate date a given daylength occurs at various latitudes within the United States (Table One).

If you know the daylength required to flower a certain plant, this table tells you when that daylength occurs naturally. Then to flower the plant early, or late, you need only to give it the proper daylength by artificial means.

Table One can be useful to us in producing early flowers for a show. For example, assume you live at 40 degrees North latitude. Your fall garden show has been scheduled for September 25 and you want to exhibit a certain chrysanthemum variety that does not normally flower until October 15. We know that chrysanthemums require a daylength of about fourteen hours to set buds, so by looking at Table One we see that a fourteen-hour daylength occurs naturally at 40 degrees North latitude on about September 1. Since our mum flowers normally on October 15, this means that it requires six weeks from the start of short days until flowering. To bring it into flower by Septem-

TABLE ONE

DAYLENGTH	LATITUDES				
	20	30	40	50	60
10 hour				Jan. 11 Dec. 1	Feb. 11 Nov. 11
11 hour			Jan. 21 Nov. 18	Feb. 11 Nov. 1	Oct. 21 Feb. 1
12 hour	Jan. 1 Dec. 11	Feb. 11 Oct. 25	Feb. 21 Oct. 15	Nov. 1 Oct. 18	Mar. 8 Oct. 11
13 hour	Apr. 1 Sept. 21	May 11 Sept. 21	Mar. 21 Sept. 21	Mar. 21 Oct. 1	Nov. 18 Oct. 1
14 hour	June 1 Aug. 1	Apr. 21 Aug. 21	Apr. 11 Sept. 1	Aug. 1 Sept. 11	Mar. 25 Sept. 26
15 hour		June 11 July 11	May 5 Aug. 11	Apr. 6 Aug. 21	Apr. 8 Sept. 11
16 hour			June 1 July 11	May 1 Aug. 11	Apr. 15 Aug. 25
17 hour				May 21 Aug. 1	Apr. 21 Aug. 18
18 hour					May 1 Aug. 11

ber 25, then, we must start short days six weeks before this date or on August 10. In actual practice it would be better to allow a week or two extra time and start short days on August 1, and if the flower comes in too early simply place it in cold storage.

ADJUSTING THE LENGTH OF DAY

We can shorten the length of day by artificially obstructing the light after the plants have received the proper photoperiod. For example, after chrysanthemums have received twelve to fourteen hours of daylight, something must be pulled over them to cut out the light, and this must be done each day until flower color begins to show. In the morning it must be removed early enough to give the plants a full twelve to four-teen-hour day.

The material that florists use to cover their plants is a black sateen cloth with a minimum of 68 by 104 threads to the inch (Post). Black building paper can be used as well, but it is more difficult to handle. In either case, the joints must be very well sealed since it takes only five to fifteen foot-candles of light to give a long day effect (Fig. 5).

Fig. 5. A shading setup for shortening the length of day.

One problem with shortening the day in the summer is the high temperature that builds up under the covering. As mentioned earlier, this high temperature can destroy flower color or even destroy the short day effect. For this reason, it would be better to shorten the day in the morning hours and let the day end naturally in the evening since temperatures are often cooler in the early morning.

To lengthen the day, incandescent light bulbs must be suspended over the plants. In other words, if we want to keep a short-day plant from flowering in order to meet a later show date, then forty-watt bulbs should be suspended over a four-foot-wide bed, the bulbs four feet apart and suspended two and two-thirds feet above the plants. As Post says reflectors should be used on the bulbs (Fig. 6).

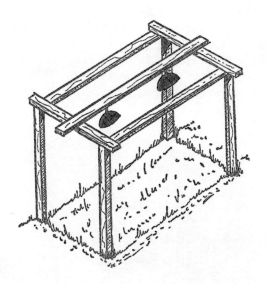

Fig. 6. A lighting setup for extending the length of day.

The lights should go on for four hours to lengthen the day. It is best to inject these four hours during the middle of the night, say from eleven to three o'clock. To keep from being awake all night an automatic time switch (which is relatively inexpensive) can be used. By having the light on during the middle of the night, the long dark period which the plant needs to produce a hormone, or whatever the sustance may be, for flowering, is broken and enough of this substance is not manufactured by the plant.

In lighting a particular crop we must always remember to prevent the light from shining over onto another adjoining bed in which the plants may have a different photoperiodic requirement. It would be wise to construct a barrier of black cloth or building paper between lighted and unlighted beds unless the neighboring plants are indifferent to photoperiod.

The manipulation of photoperiod is one way in which the blooming time of a particular flower may be changed. It may sound like a lot of work to you, but as garden showmen we must know these various points in the event that we might want to use them to our advantage.

4

Temperature

People sometimes ask which factors affecting plant growth are the most important. Soil, light, temperature, and gases are all dovetailed into a marvelous arrangement for plant growth; for this reason it is very difficult to answer since one factor cannot function properly without the other. If I were forced to give an answer, however, I would say that temperature is the most important to the garden showman, and you notice that I didn't say plant growth.

This statement is made because the garden showman, in order to be successful, must develop into a great manipulator of temperature. Raising the temperature can hasten the development of a flower to meet a show date, while lowering the temperature will retard the development of a flower. High temperatures in storage shorten the life of flowers, while low temperatures can keep a flower in prime condition for several weeks. These are the reasons why showmen must understand temperature and how to use it to their advantage.

There are so many ways in which temperature affects plant growth that this chapter, like those on soil and light, will stress only those ways that we can use to produce better exhibition material. You as a reader must not think for one minute that this is a complete discussion on how the factors affecting plant growth work; if it were, this book would be in the form of an encyclopedia of at least thirty volumes.

RESPIRATION

In the chapter on light, we discussed photosynthesis and stated that through it the plant converts water and carbon dioxide into organic compounds and oxygen using light as the source of energy. Respiration, then, is simply the reverse of photosynthesis where the plant breaks down carbohydrates to yield water and carbon dioxide. It is erroneously stated in some works that respiration occurs only at night, but actually it goes on at all times. During the day the carbon dioxide produced is used up so fast by photosynthesis that respiration is difficult to measure. In darkness, when photosynthesis is at a standstill, it is relatively easy to measure respiration and this is why some say that respiration occurs only in darkness.

We know why photosynthesis is important to us since through this process the plant produces foods. Respiration is just as important since through it the foods are broken down to be used by the plant. Just as in the case of photosynthesis, the respiration rate is increased with an increase in temperature.

Florists use this principle to good advantage in growing their crops. They try to run the day temperature 10 to 15 degrees higher than the night temperature. Simply, this means that they are trying to have the photosynthetic rate higher than that of respiration so that the food is not broken down faster than it is produced. This situation is difficult to achieve in the summer months when temperature is hard to control. In the winter, however, it is not so much of a problem.

Exhibitors will find it difficult to control the temperatures out of doors since there is no way to thermostat mother nature. But we can make good use of temperature control in lowering the respiration rate during the period between the removal of the specimen from the plant and the time it leaves the show table.

PRACTICAL TEMPERATURE APPLICATIONS

Water Temperature   It has been proved that warm water moves more quickly into a cut stem than cold water. For this reason, then, we as showmen should carry a bucket of warm, bath temperature water (110 degrees) with us when we are picking our exhibition material. I find that some showmen are more concerned as to whether they cut the stem on a slant than in using warm water into which to plunge the flower stems.

Flowers should then be left in the same bucket in an uncrowded condition and placed in a cool spot for the conditioning process. Actually a refrigerator set in the forties is ideal, but if this is not possible a cool spot on the basement floor is next best. The water then cools to surrounding temperatures, but by this time the stems have taken up sufficient quantities.

By placing our flowers, fruits, or vegetables in a cool place we are actually cutting down the respiration rate and allowing the flower to break down its organic foods more slowly, which in turn prolongs its life. The show committee should also strive to keep the show room as cool as possible even though this is difficult to do if the show is held during the summer. Most shows, however, do not last very long, so that if the exhibition material is conditioned properly it will hold up for the duration of the show.

Thirty-one Degree Storage   Often we can govern the time at which a plant will bloom or bear fruit by the date of planting or by our pinching or lighting techniques. This is not a foolproof method, however, since the weather is capable of playing tricks with our plan.

The time at which a flower blooms need not be a burdensome problem for the showman. In the early 1950s, two Cornell University floriculturists, Drs. Kenneth Post and Charles Fischer, published in Cornell Extension *Bulletin* 853, "Commercial

Storage of Cutflowers," a report on 31-degree storage. This bulletin was written for the commercial florists and it tells them how to store flowers for long periods of time without destroying the keeping quality of the flowers upon removal from storage.

After a flower is severed from the plant, it is usually stored in the absence of light and it therefore can no longer synthesize food. We will recall from our discussion of respiration that it is quite capable of breaking down the food contained in it at a rate proportionate with the temperature. When the food is completely broken down the flower "goes by." The object, then, is to store flowers at as low a temperature as possible without freezing them.

Drs. Post and Fischer point out that at 32-degrees the rate of respiration is half that at 50-degrees. They further state that at low temperatures the invasion of fungi on the flowers is diminished. Also, ethylene gas which is produced by many flowers in storage and which shortens the life of a flower is reduced below the danger point at temperatures below 40-degrees.

These investigators found the critical point to be 33-degrees. Above this temperature flower quality deteriorated in storage. It is a known fact that most flowers freeze at 29-degrees. Therefore, they picked 31-degrees, the mid-point, as an optimum storage temperature for most flowers on the basis of those which they tried.

This work has been helpful to florists. It can just as well be helpful to a garden showman, too. Many garden club members in Connecticut have tried this technique with success in a home refrigerator.

Procedure You will need a refrigerator that you can devote entirely to the storage of flowers. One that contains food is not satisfactory for 31-degree storage. Some showmen I know have purchased inexpensive used refrigerators especially for this purpose. It can double as an overflow for the kitchen refrigerator when not in use for flowers. Make sure that you select one that has a dial for setting the temperature. Then place a thermometer in it for a week or so and periodically test the temperature to make sure that it is in line with the dial setting. After a week of testing you can begin using it for its intended purpose.

Drs. Post and Fischer found that most flowers stored best if they had never been placed in water before the storage period. If for some reason the flowers wilt before you have a chance to store them, it is possible to condition them first in water and then put them up. Red roses, however, will "blue" when this is done. Try not to let flowers wilt before storing them but rather place them in the refrigerator immediately after picking.

Flowers stored at 31 degrees should be placed in either a cellophane or plastic bag. The large sizes are best for most flowers. Seal the open end with a rubber band, making sure that it is tightly closed. Paper bags or newspapers do not make good containers since they absorb moisture, according to the Cornell report (Fig. 7).

Flowers stored in this manner will last as long as flowers picked from the garden when they are finally placed on the

Fig. 7. A flower in a plastic bag all ready for 31-degree storage.

show table. Most flowers should be picked a day before the
normal show stage for 31-degree storage, and allowed to develop fully after they are removed and before they go to the
show. Lilies, however, may not develop fully after storage, so
they must be stored in full development or close to it.
Gladioli do not store well, unless, like the lilies, they are stored
in full development. This makes the storage of these flowers
difficult since spikes of both are exhibited with unopen buds.

The Cornell report listed most of the common cut flowers.
During the past few seasons, I have stored many of the common
garden flowers with success. The following is a list of both
the Cornell stored flowers and those which I tried and how
long it is safe to store them at 31 degrees and still have exhibitable material.

EIGHTEEN DAYS

Roses

TWO WEEKS

Anemone
Asters
Camellias
Cleome
Daffodils
Dicentra
Day lilies
Nasturtiums
Petunias
Phlox
Most Begonias
Lupine

THREE WEEKS

Ageratum
Alyssum

Anchusa
Columbine
Campanula
Centaurea
Cosmos
Delphinium
Foxgloves
Hollyhocks
Candytuft
Iris
Marigolds
Pansies
Peonies
Pentstemon
Pyrethrum
Rhododendrons
Snapdragons
Violets
Zinnias
Monkshood
Lilies

FOUR WEEKS

Calendulas
Carnations

FIVE WEEKS

Chrysanthemums

EIGHT WEEKS

Tulips

It should be noted here that all flowers placed in storage should be clean and free of disease as all good show material should be. Even though disease problems are not likely to be too great at so low a temperature, it is possible to have some trouble. Therefore, it is better not to tempt nature.

Handling the Flowers After Storage Upon removal from storage, place the flowers in warm water after first cutting off a portion of the base of the stem. Then put them in a cool place, such as a basement, for six to eight hours before exhibiting them. This is the minimum conditioning time. It is perfectly all right to leave them for an entire day if desired.

Raising the Temperature to Hasten Flower Development Flowers can be hastened into bloom by raising the temperature. We have already agreed that out of doors we cannot just walk over to a thermostat and accomplish this, so we have to employ other means in order to achieve our goal.

A neat cap can be made by placing a plastic bag or hot-cap over a coat-hanger frame (Fig. 8). The cap is then mounted over the flower and in so doing the temperature under the cap is raised a few degrees, thus hastening the development of the flower. This tool is especially valuable when several days of cloudy weather have slowed down development to the point where if left to nature the flower would not bloom until after the show. We can only count on the cap to hasten development by a few days.

The showman should watch conditions under the cap. If temperatures are normally on the high side, punch several

Fig. 8. The movable plastic bag method for hastening flowering.

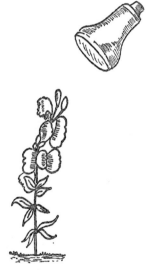

Fig. 9. The heat-lamp method for hastening flowering by raising the temperature.

holes in the plastic bag to permit a little air circulation. If this is not done the flower may actually deteriorate.

Some showmen have used a heat lamp to good advantage in hastening flower development, but this can be risky business. If the heat lamp is placed too close to the flower, scorching will occur. If you use a heat lamp place it no closer than three to four feet from the flower (Fig. 9).

Temperature and Flower Color   High temperatures will fade flower color just as much as low temperature will intensify colors. This is especially true of the reds. We have just mentioned that the showman who employs the cap technique to hasten flower development must also be on constant watch as to what is happening under the cap. In high light intensity areas the showman would be wise to use either lath or cheesecloth-covered frames to cut down on temperature associated with high light intensities. This may not be a problem with all plants, but experience will show which are the offenders. Dianthus, chrysanthemums, roses, and dahlias are but a few of the flowers that fade under high temperatures (Figs. 10 and 11).

Fig. 10. Cutting down the light intensity with a cheesecloth-covered frame.

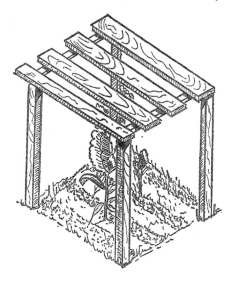

Fig. 11. Cutting down the light intensity with a lath frame.

5

Growing and Training

Growing for showing is both an art and a science. It is an art because as showmen we develop a keen sense for the best that mother nature has to offer for exhibition. It is a science in that we give mother nature a hand in producing the very best.

So far our concern has been with using nature's wonders (soil, light, temperature, water, and air) to our advantage in producing top-notch, healthy plants. This chapter deals mainly in shaping leaves, stems, flowers, and fruit into blue ribbon winners and, therefore, furthering the art and science of growing for showing.

THE SHOW GARDEN SITE

We have said much about soil and light in leading up to this chapter and have shown how soil can be improved in texture and fertility. In selecting a site for the show garden our goal must be to find a spot that is well drained. Even though we prepare the texture of the soil to the letter, proper soil aeration will be lacking if the water table is high and the area is swampy. Once our plants are in, it is very difficult to remove excess water but relatively easy to add water artificially.

58

Our second consideration in selecting a site for the show garden is to locate one that is not shaded. Trying to grow specimens under a tree canopy or under the shade of a building is a lost cause. At this point I will make a comment that has probably come to the fore of your mind many times: these points are basic to just plain good gardening.

Given these, then, we can design our garden in any shape or form we desire. Most professional show gardens are designed just like the average vegetable or cutting garden where the plants are planted in rows. Plenty of room for light penetration and air circulation and proper spacing are important. It is so easy to injure your precious specimens when cultivating or staking if they are planted too close. Tall plants like marigolds, zinnias, roses, and tomatoes must be planted a minimum of three feet apart. Medium-sized material such as asters and snapdragons should be planted two feet apart while the low-growing ageratums and dwarf marigolds take an eighteen in spacing distance. Vine crops like cucumbers and squashes, if allowed to trail on the ground, should be planted in hills four feet apart with four feet between the rows. These spacing distances, although they seem great, are just right for the production of exhibition material. If space is at a premium, then you may want to stagger your plants in a double row making them (tall group) two feet apart in each row. In other words, the plants would be zigzagged with two feet between each row and two feet between each plant in the row.

The conventional flower border planted for aesthetic effect does not offer enough space for the production of good exhibition material. Also, many of the plants grown for show are handled differently from those grown purely for aesthetic effect, mainly in the way they might be pruned or staked. If you haven't the place for a special show garden, then you may have to compromise between show garden spacing and arrangement and regular flower border design.

The layout of the show garden and its design is up to you. It can be a special garden set off by itself or at one end of the vegetable garden. You may like your garden along a fence or wall and thus serve the dual purpose of a show garden and flower border. Or you may prefer to arrange it in parklike beds as illustrated in Photograph 4. The design then is relatively unimportant as long as proper growing conditions exist.

THE QUANTITY OF PLANTS TO GROW

In judging shows I have seen so many exhibits where two out of the three flowers in a lot are uniform in size, shape, and color, but the third flower is either larger or smaller, lighter or darker than the other two. The reason for this in many instances is that the exhibitor did not grow enough material from which to select his lot.

You should grow at least nine plants of a variety and color, be these flowers or vegetables, in order to make up a lot of three uniform specimens for the show. Many schedules call for more than one specimen in a lot of certain materials, so you see the importance of growing enough from which to select. If only one specimen is needed for an exhibit, then three or four plants of this particular plant are enough.

To further stress this point, realize that it takes about one-quarter bushel of beans to select ten exhibitable pods and about one-half bushel of carrots to select three to five winners. Whether you are growing flowers, fruits, or vegetables, give yourself leeway in selection.

SHOULD YOU GROW YOUR OWN SEEDLINGS

Before we delve into this subject, a word or two might be said about variety selection for shows. It would be impossible to list all of the varieties for all of the plants which are suitable for the show table. Therefore, the important thing to stress is to make sure that you are growing a variety that has proved itself to you or to someone else as an exhibition variety.

You may see a variety that you would like to try at a

show. At most shows the name of the flower and the variety must be recorded on the entry card. If a variety is new to you but you feel that it has proved itself when grown and exhibited by someone else, this may be one that you would like to try. The important thing to remember is not to depend on too many new varieties of which you know little about as exhibition material for a show.

Exhibitors and judges used to say that the true test of a showman was to grow his material from seed to flower. This is still true, but today most people, from showman on, buy seedlings for planting at a greenhouse or garden center. In fact, it is far better to do this than to attempt to grow them under poor growing conditions.

You have no doubt gathered that show material must be expertly grown, and this applies to seedlings in the seed pan as well as plants in the garden. It is no use struggling at growing seedlings in a kitchen window or in the basement only to produce what is dwarfed or leggy, or suffering from malnutrition. No one will condemn you for realizing that you do not have the conditions for growing seedlings and buy them instead. If you are lucky enough to have a well-ventilated hotbed or greenhouse, then by all means grow your seedlings.

When you buy your seedlings, look for those that have been well grown. Select those that have grown under optimum conditions and not those that are dwarfed because of too low temperatures or lack of water or malnutrition. Know your grower and insist on plants grown in pots or bands even if they do cost a few cents more (Fig. 12). These will suffer less shock when planted and will start on their way to becoming a thrifty plant without delay.

PINCHING

Pinching means to remove the terminal growing point from the stem of a seedling. It can be done with a sharp knife or shears, but most gardeners use their thumb and forefinger.

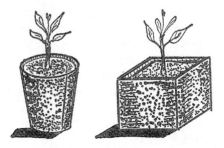

Fig. 12. The seedling on the left was started in a pot and that on the right in a band to eliminate shock in transplanting.

Fig. 13. The proper point at which to pinch.

Fig. 14. A pinched seedling.

Since the terminal shoot is dominant, its removal allows the lateral shoots to take over. Pinched plants produce, as a general rule, more shoots than non-pinched plants and this is the reason why a showman must practice pinching. Non-pinched plants produce good terminal shoots and flowers for exhibition, but when these shoots are removed there is little left for future exhibits (Figs. 13 and 14).

Not all plants require pinching. Gladioli, iris, day lilies, and lilies-of-the-valley should not be pinched since they produce flowers on their own stem or scape. Sometimes show schedules will call for a single stemmed, disbudded aster or chrysanthemum. In this case it might be wise to leave the plant unpinched and allow the terminal to grow and flower, disbudding all side shoots. A larger flower should result. Actually no flowers have to be pinched; pinching is merely a way of producing many specimens from one plant.

Pinching can be done either after a seedling becomes established in the garden or after it attains a height of eight inches. The former method is called a "low pinch" (Fig. 15) and the latter is called a "high pinch" (Fig. 16). Generally speaking, a high pinch produces earlier flowers than a low pinch.

Then there are soft and hard pinches too. A "soft pinch" is the removal of just the very tip of the terminal, while a "hard pinch" is the removal of several inches of the tip. A soft pinch produces growth of the lateral shoots more quickly than a hard pinch.

The different types of pinches are very useful as timing devices. A few plants of a variety can be pinched low, a few

Fig. 15. The "low pinch."

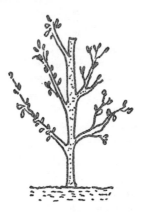

Fig. 16. The "high pinch."

Fig. 17. Pinching the laterals to delay flowering.

others high; still a few others can be pinched soft and some others hard. This, coupled with successive planting, will provide flowers in bloom, of this one variety, over a long period to meet many show dates.

Lateral shoots can be pinched too. This will delay their flowering so that you can meet still another late show. Here, too, they can be pinched high or low, hard or soft, to round out the flowering season (Fig. 17).

After pinching a plant, all of the laterals that come along

should not be left on the plant since they will crowd each other. It is true that you will have more flowers by permitting all of the laterals to develop, but this will be done at the expense of large blooms and straight stems.

Generally speaking, not more than three to five laterals should remain on the plant without risking the chance of producing inferior blooms. The removal of laterals can also be practiced in vegetables and fruit. Cucumber, melon, and squash vines should be thinned if large fruit is desired. Suckers must be removed from tomatoes to achieve the same results. And on strawberries, not more than six runners can remain on each parent plant if good, large fruit is expected.

DISBUDDING

Practically all flowers are exhibited at shows as disbuds unless the show schedule calls for a spray, as in chrysanthemums, or in the case of iris, day lilies, or lilies.

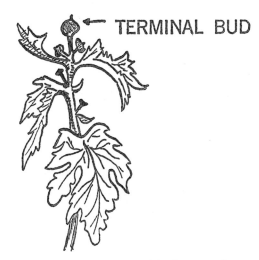

TERMINAL BUD

Fig. 18. This drawing illustrates the position of both terminal and side buds.

Disbudding means to remove all of the buds along the stem except the terminal (Fig. 18). This is done to permit the terminal to receive all of the plant's foods so that it will become large and well formed.

Disbudding cannot be done as a one-step operation. Side buds and shoots must be removed as soon as they are large enough to take hold of. Judges look for evidence of recent disbudding and they like to see specimens that have been disbudded early so that the wound has time enough to heal over.

When you disbud, make sure that you do not leave the little "bud-stem" or "hatrack." This is almost as bad as leaving the bud there too because it indicates poor care. If necessary, remove the bud and its stem with a tweezer so as not to leave the little "hatrack" behind.

STAKING FOR STRAIGHT STEMS

The flower you enter in a show must have a straight stem. Straight stems demand many points on most score cards and rightly so. This should not alarm the showman since it is quite easy to grow a straight stemmed flower.

Basic to the production of straight stems are good nutrition, proper light, and plenty of water. Given these, however, many of the flowers we grow may still produce crooked stems unless they are staked because our old friend phototropism takes over.

Staking is easy. Any kind of stake can be used ranging all the way from broom handles, sold for staking, to bamboo in all sizes. It is wise to get your stakes the winter before the show season so that you will have time to paint them. If all of the stakes in the show garden are painted uniformly they do not detract from the over-all beauty of the garden.

While with many plants it is most practical to drive the stake right into the ground next to the plant (Fig. 19), it is best to do this only with plants that produce very long stems. Plants

Fig. 19. Vertical staking.

Fig. 20. Diagonal staking.

producing medium length or short laterals might best be staked as illustrated in Figure 20. When staked in this fashion, the lower part of the stem does not produce a crook as in Figure 19 and when long stems are the object this might mean the difference of a few points, especially in keen competition. Furthermore, this type of staking has another advantage. It allows more light to enter the center of the plant. The disadvantage is that it requires a lot more space than vertical staking.

The paper or plastic-coated wire sold for tying plants is a great timesaver over the use of string. All we have to do is to cut a short piece of wire and tie the stem to the stake, repeating the process every three to four inches. It is wise to allow enough room within the tie for the stem and your little finger. This allows enough space for the growth of the stem in diameter. It is a good idea, however, to check the ties from time to time to make sure that the stem isn't girdling.

PROTECTING THE SPECIMENS FROM WEATHER DAMAGE

We have already mentioned how a mulch absorbs raindrops and therefore keeps the soil from spattering onto the leaves and flowers. But the rain itself hitting the flowers of some plants can produce blemishes. Delphiniums, petunias, roses, and dahlias are members of a group that spot badly during rains.

Just before a show, when these flowers are coming into bloom, it is a shame to have them damaged. We, therefore, must provide them with protection so that they will not spot or be burned from the wind.

The cap made by covering a coat hanger with a plastic bag, which we discussed in the last chapter, can also be used in protecting plants from storm damage. This cap can be mounted on a stake so that it can be slid up and down to protect different height flowers at different times.

Some gardeners do not believe in staking the sturdy-stemmed plants like gladioli and iris. But to me this seems like wise insurance protection from wind damage. For this reason,

I recommend staking all material in the garden as it grows so that you won't have to run around staking, and covering too, just before a storm.

A BIT OF PERSUASION

Altering flowers so that they are put together in a different way than nature intended them is a sin in the show world. By this I mean removing damaged petals, gluing a dropped petal back on, removing the bottom florets of a flower spike, or painting a recent disbud. Judges are on the lookout for this type of artistry and if any of these things are detected it means a downgrade in the exhibitor's score.

A bit of "friendly persuasion," however, is not taboo. For example, one floret of a glad spike may throw the whole spike off standard. This floret, let us say, is facing the back of the spike instead of straight forward. Or a daffodil petal may not conform with the others because it is either too reflexed or too curved.

By handling these parts gently and being very patient, they may be bent around to conform with the other flower parts. This must be done as soon as the fault is noticed or it may be difficult to do later. Since you are not removing or attaching a part of the flower, there is nothing wrong in giving nature a helping hand.

6

Battling the Pests

This would be such a wonderful gardening world if only the pests would leave our plants alone! Since they do not, we have to learn to live with them just as we do with taxes, monthly bills, and the other hardships of life.

Maintaining our plants in a healthy state is the first and best way to begin our battle of pest control. Just as with animals, if a plant is in an unhealthy state it is much more likely to succumb to disease and insect attack.

Just the slightest blemish on the foliage, flower, or fruit of a show specimen is considered very indicative of poor culture. We, therefore, must constantly be on our toes in waging our pest control battle.

SPRAY OR DUST?

This question is so often asked by gardeners. You yourself must decide which method you will use based on the pros and cons of each system.

Sprays are generally less expensive than dusts, but more time consuming to apply since they have to be mixed with water, put into a sprayer, and then the sprayer has to be thoroughly washed out after each use. Fungicidal sprays are often considered more effective than dusts because their particle size is finer than in dusts. Generally, toxicity to fungi is greater with a decrease in the particle size of the fungicide.

While dusts are generally more expensive than sprays but so much easier to apply since they require no mixing with water. Considering that no residues from pesticides should be on the show specimen once it reaches the show, dusts are usually easier to wash off the leaves and stems of the plants than spray residues. For this same reason, however, dusts are less residual on the plants out of doors under the force of rain and this is a disadvantage.

I cannot tell you which system you should use. You must draw your own conclusion based on your own situation and the ideas presented here. Hereafter, I will refer to the practice of applying pesticides to plants for pest control as spraying, but I am using the term generally to refer to either spraying or dusting. I am in no way attempting to influence you to spray rather than dust.

HOW OFTEN AND WHEN SHOULD YOU SPRAY?

This is a difficult question to answer, but generally speaking you should spray your plants every ten days to two weeks. This statement by no means suggests that after the spray is applied you can forget the matter of pests until the next "spray day." A daily inspection trip to the show garden is necessary for the garden showman not only to look for pests but to disbud, pinch, and perform all of the other developmental duties.

Heavy rains can wash sprays from the plants and this means that supplementary sprays may be necessary between the biweekly sprays. Because you should avoid getting spray material on the flower head, it may be necessary to employ the tried and true "hand-picking" method of destroying insects from the flower. Sprays have been known to discolor some flowers once they have opened.

Spraying should be done in the early morning. This is

essential for dusting, too, since natural dew should be on the plants so that the dust will adhere to the leaves. The reason for spraying in the morning is that, generally speaking, less harm can come to the plant. Spraying during the hot midday sun can cause severe burning and scorching on the foliage. We shouldn't spray in the evening because it is not wise to permit our plants to go into the dark, night period with wet leaves. As was mentioned earlier, wet conditions combined with darkness and heat favor disease invasion. Therefore, we conclude that early morning spraying, before the sun is too hot, is best.

During low light intensity periods, soft, succulent growth is produced on the plants. It is best, then, not to spray after a period of cloudy weather, for the spray material applied could possibly injure this tender growth. Allow the plants to get a whole day of sunlight before you spray them. After a sunny period, the growth is hardened.

THE IMPORTANCE OF ADEQUATE COVERAGE

The place where most gardeners fall down in the spraying of plants is on this matter of adequate coverage. If we expect good results in pest control, the lower as well as the surface of the leaf should be covered. Also we must cover the entire stem and only exclude the flower itself from being covered. When disease spores fall on a plant part, this part must be thoroughly covered with a fungicide if good control is expected. We have no guarantee as to where these spores will fall. This same principle applies in insect control.

It is a wise practice to include a spreader in your spray water when you are mixing in the wettable powder. Spreaders can be purchased at garden supply centers, but most of us have good spreaders right in our homes. Soap powders make good spreaders and if you add two teaspoons per gallon of water, the surface tension of the water will be sufficiently reduced so that the spray will not form on the leaves in tiny

Fig. 21. When a spreader is not added to a spray, droplets form and roll off the leaf.

droplets that eventually roll off (Fig. 21). Liquid detergents are not good spreaders.

We must not dwell too long over one particular plant when we spray. Too much spray applied to the foliage will only drip off and leave little residue. The object, then, is to cover a plant thoroughly and move right along.

USE CAUTION WITH PESTICIDES

Pesticides must be respected! Many of those we use are relatively harmless. Rotenone and pyrethrum are in the harmless group. Nevertheless, whether we are using rotenone or DDT, it is wise to get into the habit of handling all of these materials with utmost care. Here are six rules that should be followed carefully at all times in the use of pesticides:

1. Always read the entire label on the pesticide container and follow these instructions very carefully.
2. Use care in applying a pesticide. Children and pets should not be present during the spraying operation.

3. For your own protection always wear gloves while spraying and then take a shower or bath when the job is completed.
4. Keep pesticides out of the reach of children and under lock and key.
5. It is wise to purchase only enough spray material for one year since these materials can break down in storage and damage the plants to which they are then applied.
6. Never mix two different spray materials together unless you are sure of their compatibility. Incompatible materials will severely burn plant tissue.

ALL-PURPOSE SPRAYS OR DUSTS

All-purpose pesticides are just what the doctor ordered for the home gardener. They are combinations of insecticides and fungicides that will do the job of controlling most of your pest problems. A popular all-purpose formulation on the market contains malathion, methoxychlor, and captan. Some all-purpose materials contain additional ingredients, but at least these three are needed to control most insects and diseases of our plants.

As already stated, an all-purpose material does not control all problems. Specific controls are needed for certain pests. Malathion and methoxychlor will control most of the chewing and sucking insects and captan will control many diseases, but occasionally we run across a problem that these three do not control.

Plant pests vary to a great degree in each section of the country. For this reason it would be wise for you to consult your state experiment station for its recommendations for controlling home flower and vegetable garden pests.

1. The court of honor.

2. Everyone enjoys a garden show.

3. A rose flower possessing all of the desirable points. This blossom would be judged a blue ribbon winner.

4. The bed-type of show garden.

5. A typical gladiolus exhibit.

6. The dahlia show at the Garden Exchange.

7. Properly prepared carrots, peppers, cabbage, and potatoes exhibited typically.

8. The squash exhibit, showing also a method of staging.

9. Properly prepared melons, apples, and pears.

10. An interesting study of degrees of uniformity of size in tomato specimens. Note that the groups generally show good uniformity with the exception of the one at top right center, which is a glaring example of more uniformity.

11. The melons pictured here show the desired ribbing and webbing of a mature specimen with the exception of the one at the upper right, which is immature.

12. The apples with the leaves attached are improperly prepared for exhibition.

PART TWO

Selection

7

Potted Plants

While this book was designed primarily to deal with outdoor plants, it would be unfair to completely overlook the house plants normally grown either in the house or in a greenhouse under artificial means. There are so many different genera, species, varieties, and types of plants grown under these conditions that we will deal only with this group in a general manner—flowering plants and foliage plants—with perhaps a mention or two of a few specific plants during the discussion.

The matter of containers for potted plants for showing is basic to either group, however. I find that the type of container in which a specimen plant should be exhibited is a matter of concern to many gardeners. They wonder if a clay pot is suitable for the show table. Some gardeners decide not, evidently, for they cover clay pots with foil.

Unless the show schedule suggests a specific container, such as a planter, a dish, or a novelty receptacle, you can assume that a clean clay pot is all right for your plant to be exhibited in. It is best never to cover the pot with foil for this may indicate to the judge that you grow your plants this way, but, actually, growing plants in a foil-covered pot is a poor practice.

The pot that holds your plant must be clean regardless of its composition. Clay pots often become discolored with algae or salt deposits and are difficult to clean. For this reason it is my opinion that the relatively new plastic pots are made to order for the showman. Not only do they stay relatively clean during the culture of the plant, but they are also easy to clean if they do get dirty. Also these pots are quite decorative.

Whatever container you select, make sure that it provides for drainage and good drainage at that. This means that the pot must have holes in its bottom so that excess water can be eliminated. Both clay and plastic pots are made with this important provision in almost every case. We cannot expect to grow good specimens in a poorly drained container. Of course the soil mixture and fertilization practices are important too, as well as light and temperature.

So many specimens that are exhibited do not have a good relation between the size of the plant and its pot. Either the pot is far too large for the plant or vice versa. As a general rule, the plant, above soil level, should be twice the size of the pot if a good balance is expected. Of course this applies only to plants that grow directly upward, not to plants like African violets that grow relatively flat. This type of plant usually looks best in a four-inch three-quarter pot, meaning that the pot is four inches wide (inside diameter) and three inches deep.

FLOWERING PLANTS

Needless to say, flowering plants must be in flower at the time of exhibition. This point seems perfectly obvious, but sometimes a showman will exhibit a flowering plant when it is temporarily out of bloom and therefore his point score is drastically cut.

The size of the individual blooms should be as large as possible. Sometimes when a plant has many buds that would crowd each other anyway, you would be wise to thin them so that those remaining will develop into large, thrifty blooms, If you have a choice of a particular plant, select the one that has many visible blossoms, not one where the blossoms are down between the foliage. Flowering plants are grown so that the observer can enjoy the flowers, and the judge keeps this point in mind.

The condition and quality of the flowers must be excellent, meaning that you will have to neatly remove individual flowers as they go by. Flowers like geraniums that are borne on a stem must be removed so that no portion of the stem is still on the plant. Telltale stubs will cost the showman many valuable points.

Flower color must be uniform over a specimen plant and typical of the plant. The color, to be at its best, should be clear and bright and the flowers must be symmetrical and well formed. Faded flowers or ones that are malformed are undesirable and should be removed.

Some flowering plants are mistakenly exhibited in foliage plant classes. The coleus is a classical example since it is grown primarily for its foliar effect. Although the coleus blossom is not very attractive, the plant is technically a flowering plant. Some shows make special classes for such creatures, calling the class "flowering plants grown for foliar effect." Consult your show committee if there is any question as to where you should exhibit such plants since the show committee is the body that describes the show setup to the judge.

Cultural perfection is next in line in importance. This means that not only must the plant be in good vigor and health, but it must also be in good form and shape. Flowering plants have to be trained and pinched so that they will develop a symmetrical shape with no crowded stems that make the plant appear unbalanced. This also means that leggy, rank plants are not acceptable. These require pinching to produce lateral shoots to make them full and balanced.

So that plants will not grow one-sided, they must be turned from one-quarter to one-half turn each day to keep them from growing towards the light source. We already mentioned this point earlier, but its importance is so great in the production of show plants that it bears mentioning again.

Many plants, such as African violets, must be exhibited as single crown plants. This means that only one plant can occupy a pot and no side plants can be present. The plant must have a symmetrical arrangement of leaves with flowers extending above the foliage. Photograph 1.

It is a popular misconception among some showmen that foliage is not so important on flowering plants as in non-flowering plants. This is not true. The foliage on your plants must be a lustrous green, free of dust, and unblemished. Any yellowed leaves must be neatly removed in advance of the show, and the plant should be well filled out with leaves to give a good background to the flowers.

Finally, if you are wondering whether the fact that a certain plant is more difficult to grow than another will command special attention by the judge, the answer is "yes." Both difficult and rare plants are given special consideration by the judge when compared to a relatively easy one. This is only fair since it indicates that the showman, if he exhibits a good specimen, knows how to grow this difficult or rare specie that demands more knowhow than a common, easy-to-grow plant.

FOLIAGE PLANTS

In this group, the foliage and its condition is the all-important thing, since the plants are grown only for their leaves. A foliage plant without good green, unblemished foliage is much like a car without a motor. The showman must also attempt to produce foliage the right size for the variety. In other words, it must not be too small because of poor cultural conditions.

A good symmetrical or asymmetrical balance of foliage is important. To achieve this, the showman must give his plants good culture through proper pinching and training. Plants, like ivies, that need support must receive it in a manner that is attractive. For example, the support must be decorative without detracting from the beauty of the plant itself.

Foliage plants should be vigorous and exhibit good culture. Their leaves must shine without the use of artificial shining material. A soft flannel cloth gently rubbed over the foliage will shine the leaves beautifully without the help of artificial devices. Judges who detect the use of artificial plant shining sprays or oils should disqualify the plants from the show.

Rarity and difficulty in growing foliage plants must be considered by the judge just as much here as with flowering plants. In fact, so many people grow the tried and true foliage plants that the exhibitor who exhibits an unusual or difficult specimen should be rewarded for his efforts.

8

Garden Flowers

Certain rules are basic to the exhibiting of all garden produce. Exhibitors who follow these rules have won half of the battle before even considering the specific requirements.

You as a showman should familiarize yourself with the terms "type," "uniformity," "maturity," "freedom from damage," "substance," and "cultural perfection." These are the bywords of all showmen and judges.

TYPE   All specimens shown should be true to type. The type of flowers, fruits, and vegetables will be discussed in the following pages, but basically, when you are exhibiting a snapdragon, make sure that the flower spike is long and tapered rather than short and clubby. A clubby snapdragon is not true to type. Cucumbers with curled ends are not true to type either, nor is a one-sided apple.

UNIFORMITY   When you hear this word used, it refers to the uniformity of size, shape, and color. If your show schedule calls for a single specimen, then your main obligation is to show one that is true to type. But a large percentage of the produce shown must be in lots of three or five. When this is the case all three of the lot members should be uniform in every respect. Let us take zinnias as an example. It is relatively easy to find three zinnias of the same diameter, but it becomes more of a problem to select three of the same depth of flower head. Even within a variety this is hard. The judge, if you have ever watched one, will look at the specimens from the top down and then turn and look at them from the side to make sure that they conform in size in every respect. Each zinnia specimen should be of the same shape. Keep the typical type in mind and select all of the specimens that conform in shape to this type. I have seen zinnias shown that were uniform in size, but one specimen had more petals on one side which thus changed the shape. This specimen was not only off in shape but also in type.

It is best not to show at all than to show atypical material. However, I have seen exhibited three flowers in a lot that were perfect in size, color, maturity, and every other respect except that they were all one-sided. In this case a judge has to admit that the exhibitor knows the cardinal rules of judging, but has to mark him down on type rather than uniformity of shape, even though the flowers are all shaped the same way. So you see, these points are intricately involved.

Unless the show schedule calls for a lot of three flowers in mixed colors you had better make sure they are uniform in color. Some judges allow much leeway in this respect, but most judges will mark off points if the flowers within a lot are not of the same color.

It is taken for granted that exhibitors know that all members of a show lot should be of the same variety. And yet I have run into so many exhibits in which two members of a lot are of one variety and the third member of another. When a judge spots this he looks no further. This automatically means "no award."

MATURITY All produce exhibited should be mature. Zinnias that have not fully opened should not be shown, nor should marigolds, dahlias, or any other produce. Often a show schedule will specify a class of immature material such as green tomatoes or strawflowers. This is done especially when a show is early for late maturing material. Unless a show schedule specifies that it is all right to show immature material, never assume that you can pass the critical eyes of the judge if you do.

Perhaps more of a problem is the showing of overmature specimens. This is so easy to do when you have planned to show a certain product and because of warm weather it came along too fast. However, don't downgrade your reputation as a showman by showing overmature material. A large percentage of points will be taken off by the judge when he sees a dahlia with curled, browning lower petals or a tomato where the skin has begun to shrivel. If you don't have the facilities to store the specimens at 31 degrees you are better off to cancel that entree.

There are two general rules that you can follow in determining whether or not your material is at the right stage of maturity. For the round-headed flowers such as marigolds, zinnias, dahlias, and the like, the flowers should be opened enough so that the outer petals begin to turn down and are still in good fresh condition. For the spike-type flowers, such as gladioli, snapdragons, and salvia, as many of the florets on the spike should be open as possible without the bottom ones overmature or having fallen off.

FREEDOM FROM DAMAGE   This term refers to many points. Mechanical injury is one of them. Mechanical injury refers to any type of damage on a specimen made by man or machine. If we are not careful in picking the product we can injure a leaf stem, or fruit. Also, most of the mechanical injury is caused in transit from the garden to the show. The last chapter of this book discusses the transportation of material to the show in a way to avoid damage.

Another type of damage is caused by insects or diseases. I, as one judge, see red when a specimen shows evidence of pest attack. This to me means not only that the exhibitor has poor gardening practices but that he has no business trying to exhibit his inferior material. Most judges will agree on this point.

Spraying or dusting will control pests, but evidence of pesticide residue on the foliage, flower, or stem will take off many points from your score. Chapter 6 goes into this subject in detail, so there is no further need to discuss it here.

Soil or dirt on the specimen is inexcusable. Judges will deduct many points from the total score. Fortunately this is not too much of a problem at shows. It will occur more often on vegetables than on other produce since so many of the vine crops grow on the ground. But on crops like petunias, verbenas, and the other low-growing plants, it can be a problem. A mulch on the show garden floor will eliminate most of the rain spatter of soil onto the plants and the remainder can be washed off.

SUBSTANCE   A flower with good substance is turgid. This means that it is not wilting, that the cells within the plant are full of water, and that the specimen will hold up well on the show table. Also a flower of good substance is at the peak of maturity as discussed above. So often the exhibitor will select a flower of good substance in the garden, but through improper hardening and pre-show table preparation the specimen deteriorates in substance. If your specimen is not tall, erect, turgid, and glistening, do not enter it in the show.

CULTURAL PERFECTION   An exhibit that shows signs of nutrient deficiencies, crooked or weak stems, flowers placed at an improper angle on the stem, weather-spattered areas on the leaves or flowers, foliage burn due to high light intensities or sprays, bleached areas on the under side of the fruit, or sunburn, as well as countless other defects, lacks cultural perfection. In other words, this means that the gardener did not give the specimen the culture it needed to develop into a blue ribbon entry.

Most of this text deals with cultural perfection, and ways to develop as perfect a specimen as mother nature will allow.

You will realize that these seven points of type, uniformity, maturity, freedom from damage, substance, and cultural perfection are closely dovetailed. The line where one point ends and the other beings is very dim and indefinite. The important thing to remember, as was mentioned in the first paragraph of this chapter, is that if these points are followed carefully, half of the battle is won before the crop in question is even judged.

SPECIFIC CROPS

The flowers to be discussed in the following pages will be divided into two main categories. We will call the flowers that produce a spike "spike form" flowers and those that do not, "round form" flowers.

Spike Form Flowers   Besides the points mentioned already in this chapter, there are a few other rules that are basic to the selection of all spike form flowers for the show table. Your object should be to select as long a spike with as many open florets as possible and still have the very bottom florets in perfect condition. In other words, the basal should show no signs of overmaturity in the form of browning around the edges, shriveling, or fading of color. You will find that this is one of the first considerations the judge gives a spike form flower.

The spike should be straight and the stem that supports it just as straight, and strong enough to support the weight of the flower head. If this book dealt with the production of flowers for arrangement it might tell you that crooked spike form flowers are desirable; since it deals with the production of horticultural specimens for show purposes we cannot overstress the importance of straight stems and spikes.

We have already mentioned the importance of disbudding the secondary side spikes from a developing primary spike and that this operation must be performed as soon as the secondary spike appears rather than when it has grown for some time. Since this is such an important point to the exhibition of spike form flowers we have mentioned it here again.

COCKSCOMB Both the crested cockscomb (*Celosia cristata*) and the plume cockscomb (*Celosia plumosa*) are popular at shows today. Either of these species can be grown easily in the garden in properly prepared soil. Here is a plant, however, that would indicate the absence of good rich soil and plenty of moisture. Drying out of the roots can cause leaf drop in cockscomb, which of course is detrimental in the production of show specimens.

DELPHINIUMS Hybrids of *Delphinium elatum* are popular flower and garden show entrees. Although this flower is normally in bloom by the time most shows come around, Post tells us in his *Florist Crop Production and Marketing* that specimens can be forced by subjecting the plants to low temperatures either in a cold frame or refrigerator for about eight weeks and then bringing them into a greenhouse for development. He further states that when forcing is begun in February flowers can be expected in April.

The American Delphinium Society has set up the following floret classes for its plant:

1. *Single*—One row of sepals and at least five petals forming the eye.
2. *Semidouble*—Two rows of sepals—eyes present or absent.
3. *Double*—More than two rows of sepals—eyes present or absent.

The term "eye" is used in reference to the center of the floret. You as a showman will want to know this classification, especially if the show is scheduled according to it.

The society also points out that there are four different types of spike forms:

1. *Column massive*—only slightly tapering.
2. *Column slender*—a slender spike but still tapered only slightly.
3. *Conical, broad.*
4. *Loose, open.*

Also the American Delphinium Society has thirteen different color classifications for its flower. You as a showman need not concern yourself greatly with these color divisions except to make sure that the specimen you exhibit is clear and definite in color whether your specimen is a bicolored or blended-type delphinium.

FOXGLOVE   I know of no classification of spikes for *Digitalis purpurea*, the foxglove. Therefore, all that can be stated here is to select long, strong, and straight disbudded spikes with as many flowers open as possible and with the bottom florets in prime condition.

Since foxgloves self-sow quite readily, the showman should be warned against growing these self-sown seedlings for show purposes. You are better off to use new seed for the production of show specimens.

GLADIOLUS   Problems arise with northern gardeners in making this popular flower bloom early enough for early garden shows. Pure gladiolus shows are scheduled late enough to accommodate most gardeners; mixed shows, however, sometimes include gladioli in their schedules and the show may be too early for some gardeners who exhibit this flower.

Dr. Post tells us that if we store our gladiolus corms at the normal 30- to 40-degree temperatures and then remove them a month before planting time to a temperature of 70 degrees, earlier flowering will result. He further states that corm size influences flowering time. In general the larger corms flower earlier than the smaller ones. By selecting various-sized corms of one variety the flowering range can be spread from two to twenty-one days. Also, the depth of planting also influences flowering time since deep-planted corms (six inches) flower later than shallow-planted corms (three to four inches).

For only a slight charge, the North American Gladiolus Council offers a fine booklet called *A Selected List of Gladiolus Varieties for Show Purposes.* The serious glad enthusiast should obtain a copy of this booklet.

Because most gardeners are growing gladiolus of the formal type, the formal and informal classification of blooms is not stressed as much today. However, we should discuss it here since it helps most showmen to see a division of gladiolus types. In the *Report* of the Committee of Judging of the New England Gladiolus Society, Incorporated we are told that the formal type should have a side-by-side arrangement of florets with one side slightly above the other. This means that the top of the bottom floret of one row should be level with the center of the bottom floret of the opposite row (Fig. 22). The sides of the spike rows should have only slight indentations in them and not great "holes."

Fig. 22. A formal gladiolus type.

In the informal types, the florets are alternated up the stem. There should be enough space between the florets to give a feeling of airiness and graciousness, but in this case, too, the indentations must not be too large.

The report further indicates that the color of gladiolus must be clear and free of flecks. If there is any variation of color in the floret it is more desirable to have the darker area around the outer portion of the floret with the lighter color in its throat. The florets should be attached snugly to the stem with as little overlapping as possible. The open florets must be uniform in shape and color and in the number of petals.

There are ideal spikes for the particular classes of gladiolus. The showman would be wise to familiarize himself with these ideals:

		MIMIMUMS		
	SIZE	*Total Buds*	*Open Flts.*	*Buds Colored*
Miniatures	Florets under 2½"	13	3–5	3–4
Small	2½ to 3½"	15	5–8	4
Medium	3½ to 4½"	16–19	5–8	4–5
Large	4½ to 5½"	18–22	6–10	5
Giant	5½ and up,	19–20	6–8	4–5

The stem length of the last three classes should be at least twenty inches. See Photograph 5.

LUPINE   *Lupine polyphyllus* can be forced in the same manner as delphiniums, but it usually flowers early enough to meet most early show dates. In fact the problem is most often one of holding lupine for a short period of time.

In this day when there are so many fine lupine varieties on the market, the showman who attempts to use old varieties may be "missing the boat." Your own seedlings should not be depended upon unless you have seen them bloom in past years. During the second year when the seedlings flower, prune out all but three of the flower spikes so that these will develop fine large florets and strong spikes. As mentioned earlier, disbud any secondary spikes that may appear.

Although many of the modern hybrids are more columnar all the way to the tip of the spike, try to select a spike that possesses a tapered tip. A good judge will realize the habits of the new types, however, so this should not be a point of major concern as long as all members of a lot are uniform. A common fault of lupines is curled tips and the showman should try to avoid this. Even after the specimens are picked they are apt to turn toward the light if they are not covered with paper as discussed in Chapter 10.

PENTSTEMON Good, clear color and high floriferousness are the prime considerations of this plant beyond those already mentioned for spike form flowers.

SALVIA The pointers mentioned for spike form flowers apply to this flower as well, but I find that the hasty showman sometimes exhibits specimens in which the actual floret has dropped and only the colored calyx remains. This is easy to do unless we study the spike. When only the calyx is present and the floret has dropped, the judge realizes that the specimen is overmature.

SNAPDRAGONS (*Antirrinium majus*) Even though snapdragons are easy to grow, the matter of selecting a good show specimen is not quite so easy. Some snapdragon spikes are clubby and short rather than long and tapered. These must be avoided. Other spikes may not have a well-filled spike but instead have many skips. Spikes with skips present might best be left at home.

The snapdragon is a classical example of a plant that definitely must be staked, pinched, and disbudded if good results are expected. You will see the best example of crooked and contorted stems and flower spikes when they are not. I know of no plant that is easier to grow and more willing to produce good exhibition material when proper cultural practices are employed.

Round Form Flowers Just as in spike form flowers, there are a few peculiarities of round form flowers that we must take into consideration before going into the specific members of the group.

The matters of overmaturity and immaturity seem to be quite a problem with this group. In exhibiting round form flowers, a good general rule to remember is that in most cases the outer petals reflex gracefully. The center petals must not be so tight and immature as to be green, but they should be tighter than the outer petals. When the outer petals begin to shrivel and fade in color, this is your signal that the flower is overmature and that it should be discarded rather than exhibited.

AGERATUM *Ageratum houstonianum* must be pinched and the lateral shoots developed into show specimens. Only three to four laterals should be left on the plant, instead of as many as will come in common culture, so that these few will develop into large ones for showing.

These lateral shoots are best when they are disbudded, leaving only the terminal flower cluster. In some varieties little disbudding is necessary, while in others considerable time must be spent at this task.

Ageratums can be kept in continuous production for show purposes if they are not all planted at the same time. A few plants can be set out initially and then when these are pinched, the "pinchings" may be rooted in any of the common rooting media and planted for successive blooming.

Ageratums fade in color quite easily. The judge will tolerate neat removal of faded flowers providing the over-all shape and form of the specimen is not destroyed. In any case, never exhibit faded or overmature material.

ASTERS   *Callistephus chinensis* are responsive to day-length. The showman who must meet an early show date can bring asters into flower according to a plan outlined by Post in his afore-mentioned work. In areas north of 35 degrees North latitude, seeds of asters may be sown in March indoors, and after they are large enough to remove from the seed flat they should be subjected to an additional four hours of artificial light, from March 20 to May 1, for blooming in late June after they are set out in the garden.

Most shows, falling on early dates, will not schedule asters, but in late summer shows asters are popular entries. Good color, straight stems, deep blossoms, and mature specimens should be selected for exhibition, and the stems should be disbudded permitting only one flower per stem.

CALENDULA   *Calendula officianalis* also should be exhibited on a disbudded stem with only the one exhibition terminal flower present. The center of the flower must be closed instead of fully opened so that the disk florets do not show.

A problem with calendulas is weak stems, but if the plants are properly grown this fault will not trouble you.

CHRYSANTHEMUM   So much has been said as to the daylength requirements of *Chrysanthemum morifolium* that it is not neces-sary to discuss them here. Therefore, we will dwell in this chap-ter on the selection of flowers for exhibition.

Chrysanthemums are exhibited either as "single stem dis-buds" or as "sprays" depending upon the schedules. Most shows provide for both types, but the disbuds are the more popular and rightly so. There are many types of chrysanthemums and they are classed as follows:

Division A

SECTION 1—*Disk conspicuous*

1. Single
2. Semidouble
3. Regular anemone
4. Irregular anemone

SECTION 2—*Ray petals incurved*

5. Pompom
6. Regular or Chinese incurve
7. Irregular incurve

SECTION 3—*Ray petals reflexed*

8. Reflexed or decorative pompom
9. Decorative or aster-flowered reflex
10. Regular or Chinese reflex
11. Irregular or Japanese reflex

Division B

12. Spoon-single
12a. Semidouble and double spoon
13. Quill
14. Thread
15. Spider

This classification by the National Chrysanthemum Society may help the showman to understand a similar division on the show schedule.

The individual blooms of chrysanthemums must be deep and the centers of the bloom well developed. Immature green centers are not permissible. The color of the flower will be a matter of high consideration by the judge. He will look for bright, clear color with petals devoid of streaks or flecks.

DAHLIAS Dahlias are short-day plants and this is why they flower naturally so late in the season. The showman who wants to enter a dahlia in an early show must shorten the day to make it flower just as with chrysanthemums, making sure that he has allowed sufficient long days for adequate vegetative growth.

For best results, dahlias should be pinched after they have grown and produced four to six nodes. The laterals that arise should be thinned to not more than three per plant and disbudded so that they only produce one flower per stem. To prolong the flowering of a single plant, part of the laterals can be pinched again.

Dahlias, too, are classified into twelve types by the American Dahlia Society. These are singles, orchid flowering, collarette, anemone, peony, incurved cactus, straight cactus, semi-cactus, informal decorative, formal decorative, ball, and pompom dahlias.

The society lists many points that the showman should follow in selecting an exhibition specimen from which the following were selected.

The color of dahlias must be clear and lustrous. Blooms that have faded or have any blemishes that affect the color are heavily marked down by the judge. The form of the flower is of utmost importance too. The center of the bloom should be round and tight. This indicates that the bloom will develop further for continued beauty. However, the center should not be green since greenness indicates immaturity.

A center that is too depressed or too high in relation to the rest of the bloom will count against your score. It should be so that the ray florets arise at a graceful angle, but the center and these florets must not look like two distinct parts mechanically put together.

The over-all blossom must be symmetrical. Lopsided or shallow flowers are bad faults as well as asymmetry caused by the absence of petals, resulting in holes in the bloom. The flower should be attached to the stem so that the angle formed by the base of the flower and the stem is about 45 degrees.

Flowers that face straight upward or downward are undesirable.

The stem should be straight and strong and in proportion to the size of the flower. The distance between the calyx of the flower to the first set of leaves should be at least the same as the diameter of the flower but not more than one and one-half this diameter. See Photograph 6.

DAY LILIES *Hemerocallis* fall into three blooming groups—early, mid-season, and late—so the showman can have blooms over a long period by selecting and growing members from each group. The showman should remember that day lilies stay open for only one day, so he must grow enough to have a wide selection. When putting day lilies into 31-degree storage, you should pick them the day before they are to bloom.

The American Hemerocallis Society gives several interesting pointers for the showing of day lilies. They state that the showman should select a scape for exhibition with as many open flowers as possible. Those scapes with many open flowers will be judged over the ones having just one. It is permissible to have a few flowers that have dropped from the scape.

Some shows provide classes for the exhibition of flowers that have been removed from the scape. This should not be done, however, unless the show in which you plan to participate has such a class.

Broken flowers or those with pollen removed are considered poor. This is true of so many flowers, but the Hemerocallis Society specifically states this in its rules. The scape supporting the flowers must not exceed thirty-six inches and they must be in proportion to the flowers as far as height and thickness are concerned.

IRIS Bearded iris can be divided into three groups—dwarf, intermediate, and tall. The stalks of dwarf iris should be not more than fifteen inches in length, while those of the intermediate group can range from fifteen to twenty-eight inches. The tall group can possess stalks exceeding twenty-eight inches according to variety.

You should select a stalk for exhibition that has as many open flowers as possible, with alternating branching so that the blossoms do not crowd or hide each other. The blossom itself must possess good form and proportion. The standards can be pointed, rounded, domed, or closed according to variety while the falls can be arched, flaring, horizontal, rounded, or strapped. No one form is better than another except that it must enhance the beauty of the flower and each part must be consistent with a particular form. In other words, one fall cannot flare while another is horizontal. They must be uniform.

LILIES Some species of lilies are more difficult to raise than others. The judge will realize this and make allowances, but the showman must consider the following points recommended by the North American Lily Society.

The showman should select a stem of lilies with as many flowers open as possible. The lowermost flowers should be open and in prime condition. Flower placement on the stem is important and the flowers should spiral vertically up the stem so that they do not interfere with one another.

The anthers should be left in the flowers unless the specimen is to be shipped a great distance. The society suggests their removal under such conditions rather than having the pollen spot the petals. Each petal must be in good condition and have good substance, not wilted, shriveled, or bruised.

Fading of color is common with some lilies either because of age or high light intensity. Lily specimens must be protected if you detect color deterioration due to bright, intense sunlight.

The form of the individual flower must be typical of the standard for the variety in question. Flower parts should be uniform in their respective arrangement and no part can be out of line with the rest. For example, a twisted or malformed petal can throw the whole specimen off many points.

MARIGOLDS AND ZINNIAS   Marigolds and zinnias are quite similar in their requirements for selection so that they have been grouped here for purposes of discussion. The word "marigolds" refers to the entire genus *Tagetes*, including African and Dwarf marigolds; the word "zinnia" refers to the entire genus also. Shows should divide the various popular species into individual classes, however.

Both zinnias and marigolds must be well developed and possess depth of bloom. In the case of marigolds, the disk florets must not be evident. If they are it means that the specimen is overmature. The outer petals of the flowers should be reflexed and these petals must still have good substance. The color of the blooms, as in every other flower, must be bright, clear, and true to variety.

NARCISSUS   Daffodils are classed into eleven divisions. Trumpet, large cupped, small cupped, double, triandrus, cyclamineus, jonquilla, tazetta, poeticus, species and miscellaneous narcissi comprise this classification. Show schedules may or may not follow this classification, but classes should be provided for at least the first four divisions.

Daffodils for exhibit must be at their prime with glistening, well-substanced petals. These petals, or perianth parts, can be flat, slightly reflexed, or slightly overlapping according to the above divisions, but each perianth member must be consistent with the other in form and position. The color within the perianth must be uniform throughout. The trumpet must be uniform in shape and in balance with the perianth.

The flower head should either be attached to the stem at a right angle or tilt slightly upward but never downward, except in the triandrus division and some of the species where this is desirable and typical. Flowers that point directly upward are not worthy of exhibition.

At least two leaves should accompany each flower exhibit. This gives the judge an indication of the general appearance and culture of the plant.

PEONIES   Peonies are classed into five main types—singles, doubles, Japanese, and anemone. These types are often the basis for flower show classes.

The condition, form, color, and size of your peony specimen will demand most of the judge's consideration. Color must be bright and typical to the variety, and size, too, varies with the variety. In addition to these points, the American Peony Society states that the stem and foliage of peonies must be of good substance and free from disease. Stems should be fifteen inches long or slightly less.

Fragrance is not placed above the other factors with peonies since some very good varieties are not fragrant. In varieties which are supposed to be fragrant, the judge may use fragrance in breaking a tie.

Although foliage is important, when specimens are kept in storage they are not penalized for slightly poor leaves. I feel that this is a step in the right direction since it is difficult to keep foliage in prime condition over the storage period.

PETUNIAS   Petunias are popular entries at flower and garden shows, the reason being that practically every home flower garden has petunias in it.

This flower is relatively easy to exhibit, but there are a few common faults made by showmen. In making up a lot of three to five specimens, whichever the schedule requests, be careful to select blooms of the same variety and color unless the schedule permits otherwise. As soon as the flowers go by on the stem, make sure to remove it along with the little stem at its base. So many exhibitors leave this flower stem on the main stem, which costs them points. Petunias, in my opinion, should be exhibited as single stem disbuds, but some show schedules also permit sprays.

Petunias self-sow around the garden and many specimens that appear on the show table are poor varieties. Be certain that you exhibit good varieties that have flowers symmetrical in form and clear in color according to the variety.

The leaves on your petunia specimen should be in good condition. Most petunia flowers are so striking that some exhibitors fail to see beyond the flower to inspect the foliage. Remember that the judge has many specimens to look over and that in most cases he has to get down to fine points, such as the small leaves of your petunia.

ROSES The American Rose Society specifies that blooms of teas, climbing teas, hybrid teas, climbing hybrid teas, hybrid perpetuals, and climbing hybrid perpetuals must be exhibited as disbudded specimens. Side buds will cost the exhibitor points. Single hybrid teas like Dainty Bess and Innocence; and polyanthas, hybrid polyanthas, floribundas, and climbers (other than those mentioned above) may be exhibited as naturally grown without disbudding.

It is hard to describe just what stage is best for exhibiting roses as far as development is concerned. Generally speaking, according to the society, the bloom should be one-half to three-quarters open. The center should be well formed, and more than just one row of the outer petals must be unfolded. See Photograph 3.

Garden showmen must avoid specimens that are dull in color or that possess split centers or malformed petals. The stems must be strong enough to support the flower but not out of proportion to it.

TULIPS Garden tulips fall into the following classification prepared by the Royal Horticultural Society and the General Dutch Bulb Growers Society.

Early Flowering
1. Duc Van Thols
2. Single Earlies
3. Double Earlies

Midseason Flowering
4. Mendels

5. Triumph

May-Flowering
6. Cottage
7. Dutch Breeders
8. English Breeders
9. Darwins

9a. Darwin Hybrids	13. Broken Cottage
10. Broken Dutch Breeders	14. Parrots
11. Broken English Breeders	15. Late doubles
12. Rembrandts	16. Species

The texture and substance of the blooms, their size, their color, and the length and strength of the stem are the prime considerations for tulips. Each flower part must be well formed and properly attached with the color clear, distinct, and true to variety. A common fault of tulips is that the stem is not strong enough to support the heavy flower. The exhibitor should select only those specimens that do possess straight, long, and stiff stems in proportion to the flower.

VIOLAS

Pansies   Since the pansy (*Viola tricolor*) and garden violets are all violas we have lumped them together in this proper heading.

Pansy flowers must have good coloring. By this we mean that the color contrast must be good and the eye of the flower clearly evident. The typical "face" associated with pansies should be apparent.

Pansies with small blossoms are not considered as good today as those with larger blossoms since so much has been done with the development of hybrids in this flower. It is true that some varieties are smaller than others, but the judge will know this and consider the point. The newer hybrids generally have a good petalage with fine substance. This is a strong point in the exhibition of pansies. Flowers that have flabby, weak, and poor substanced petals do not rate highly when judged.

A common fault of pansies is weak stem owing to poor culture. If pansies are managed properly and given enough space, this should not be a problem.

Violets   The same general factors that result in a prize-winning specimen of pansies can also apply to violets, except for coloration patterns. Violets should be fragrant, large, strong stemmed, clearly and brightly colored, and possess good substance.

9

Vegetables and Fruit

Many garden showmen consider the growing and preparation of vegetables and fruit for shows to be a much easier task than the growing of flowers or potted plants. I strongly feel that this is a matter of opinion, however, because it certainly is no easy job to select a plate of ten beans that are uniform in size, shape, or color, nor is it easy to come up with a plate of five uniform carrots without digging at least one-half bushel.

Just as in the selection of flowers for the show table, in selecting vegetables we should remember the bywords of uniformity of size, shape, and color. Also when a variety of fruit has a pink cheek, the size, shape, and degree of pinkness of the cheek should be the same in all five specimens that make up an exhibition plate. Where a single specimen is exhibited, as in melons or eggplant, this specimen must be true to type.

Many exhibitors fail to read the show schedule before they select their produce for the show. Although schedules for fruits and vegetables are similar, they may vary depending upon the show. Some shows may call for a quart of strawberries, while others may require only a pint. Others demand a quart of plums, while in some shows ten plums make up an exhibit.

Therefore, the importance of reading the show schedule carefully cannot be overstressed.

Varieties, just as in flowers, must not be mixed in a single exhibit. Regardless of how good the material is in other respects, the judge is forced to disqualify any exhibit of mixed varieties unless the show schedule specifically calls for this mixture. This seems like a very easy point to remember and yet it is violated often at shows because when the showman goes into the garden he sometimes is faced with the need to select five uniform specimens and only four can be found. He therefore includes the fifth specimen of another variety thinking that the judge will not catch this substitution. I will admit that in some instances he might be able to fool the judge, but in most cases the judge will fool him.

We have already spent considerable time discussing the matters of trueness to type, uniformity, quality, condition, maturity, cultural perfection, freedom from pests, and cleanliness of the specimens in relation to flowers. These pointers are just as true for fruits and vegetables as they are for flowers; therefore, instead of repeating this information, we will refer you to Chapter 8.

We should, however, say a word or two about the cleaning of vegetables. Dirty specimens are scored down heavily at a show and for this reason we must do a careful job of cleaning them. In Chapter 10 we do go into this in a general way, but at this point it would be wise to mention which vegetables are washed and which are not. All root crops, such as carrots and beets, and other underground specimens, like potatoes, must be washed but not scrubbed. Scrubbing leaves marks on the specimen which will cost you points at the show, and also moisture escapes through these gashes, which shortens the show life of the produce.

Leaf crops, like chard, lettuce, and cabbage, are merely hosed to remove spattered soil or spray residues. Cucumbers, squash, melons, peppers, tomatoes, and beans can be cleaned with a moist, clean cloth. These should not be submerged in water and washed.

With fruit, be careful not to remove the natural bloom on grapes, plums, blueberries, and apples. Some judges say that it is all right to shine apples with a cloth, but others say that the fruit should have its natural bloom present. If you are in doubt, leave the bloom on. Incidentally, the term "bloom" in this case refers to the white cutinous substance that covers many of the mentioned fruits.

The soft fruits, like strawberries and raspberries, cannot be washed or cleaned with a cloth. In this case, soil can be removed by brushing the fruit gently with a painter's brush. In a strawberry patch, a mulch can prevent much of the soil spatter on the fruit.

With these few introductory remarks, we are now ready to discuss specific crops and their preparation. In order to have a systematic arrangement of these crops, I have divided them into groups after the plan in H. C. Thompson's *Vegetable Crops*, published by McGraw-Hill, fourth edition, 1949.

Perennial Crops ASPARAGUS Asparagus must be in prime condition at the time of the show. It is not a common class in show schedules because it is so early maturing. Exhibitable stalks must be green in color throughout and show no purplish discoloration. A little bit of white at the butt end is permissible. These stalks should be at a "snapping" stage, which indicates that they are just right for eating. A one-inch diameter at the butt with the stalks six to eight inches long is ideal and this must be uniform in the stalks making up the exhibit, which usually is ten to twelve stalks. Colored rubber bands are used to hold the bunch together. One band should be below the tip and another a few inches above the butt ends. All spears, besides being uniform in color and size, must be round and symmetrically shaped; twisted or malformed spears are not good.

RHUBARB Exhibitable stalks of rhubarb should be firm, crisp, tender, and at the right eating stage. Usually stalks approaching one inch in diameter and ten to twelve inches long are just right for the show table. Color is extremely important with this crop and this color must be a clean, clear red throughout. Usually six stalks make up an exhibit and these must be uniform in size, shape, and color. The stalks are held together with rubber bands as with asparagus. The basal husks must be removed, but the rest of the basal portion left in tact. On the leaf end, all but two to three inches of the leaf blade should be cut off and the remaining portion cut in a fanlike fashion.

Greens CHARD The manner in which chard is exhibited depends a great deal on the show and its schedule. Some schedules call for an entire plant of chard. Others want just ten cut leaf blades and their stalks. If your show requires the entire plant, then it should be dug from the garden, all rootlets removed and the taproot washed and thoroughly cleaned. The chard should be at the proper eating stage when it is exhibited and the taproot placed in a jar of water.

Shows that ask for cut stalks and leaf blades make your selection job somewhat easier. Usually the schedule will call for ten stalks with leaf blades attached and these ten stalks must be uniform in size, shape, and color. The stalks are placed in a jar of water on the show table unless the schedule suggests something different. As in all other crops, the leaves and stems of chard must be clean and free of pest and mechanical blemishes.

SPINACH Again in the case of spinach, schedules will vary in the way in which they want you to exhibit it. Some shows prefer that you exhibit a prescribed number of cut sprigs. Others require from one to three entire plants cut at the crown, or the point where the root system begins at the base of the plant. Whichever the case may be, it is your duty to exhibit specimens at the right stage for eating and those which are a good clean

and green color. No blemishes are allowed, and wilted specimens are scored down. For this reason if you cannot exhibit
this plant in a jar of water, make sure that you carry it to the
show in water so that it will not be wilted when placed on the
show table. In the case of cut sprigs, make sure that they
are uniform in size and shape. When exhibiting entire plants,
be certain that the plant is well leafed out from top to bottom.

Salad Crops LETTUCE Many show schedules merely list one
class for lettuce, but it would be better if four classes were
offered to cover head lettuce, butterhead (such as Bibb), leaf
lettuce, and romaine. All you as an exhibitor can do is follow
the schedule as listed.

Heads of lettuce must be firm, fresh, and at the proper
stage of maturity for eating. The head must be in good condition with most of the outside or "wrapper" leaves intact. It is
improper to peel off all of the wrappers, but a few of the very
outer ones may be blemished and therefore should be removed.
Do not remove these, however, until you reach the show, for
they will protect the head in transit.

The stem or butt of the lettuce head should be neatly
squared off with a knife, leaving it about one-half inch long.
Broken or crooked cuts on the stem detract from the over-all
appearance of the head.

Heads of Bibb-type lettuce must be symmetrical, full, clean,
unblemished, and rich in color. The loose head can be severed
from the root system just above the ground line. This is also true
of leaf lettuce and romaine.

CELERY A specimen of celery is not just one stalk but rather
than entire plant. Simply dig the plant and trim off all roots
and then shape the butt, tapering it to a point. Although size
is not of utmost importance in exhibiting celery, the plant
must be at the proper maturity for eating and the heart well
developed. Uniformity of color and size in the outer stalks is

important as is shape. Twisted or malformed stalks only cost points on your score card.

Split stalks are common in celery and you as a showman must select a bunch devoid of this fault. Also, be sure to go over the bunch carefully and remove all dirt or soil that may have spattered onto the plant during a recent storm. All foliage must be left on the specimen and not pruned off as some exhibitors mistakenly have done.

PARSLEY Again we have a plant for which schedules differ in their exhibit requirements. Some shows ask for a potted plant of parsley. If this is the case it means that you have to dig the plant and pot it several weeks before the show so that it will recover from transplanting in time for the show. If your show demands a potted plant, select a thrifty, well-colored, symmetrical plant for the show. Trim off any leaves close to the crown that have yellowed or dried. And, of course, be sure to remove all dirt in the curls of the leaf, if you are showing a curled leaf variety.

Other shows require that you exhibit an entire plant unpotted in a jar of water. Here you merely dig the plant the day of the show, remove all of the rootlets, leaving the main root in a cleaned condition. The requirements concerning the top of the plant are the same as for a potted specimen.

It is the trend at most shows to schedule parsley as cut sprigs. Few shows get up separate classes for curled- and straight-leaved varieties. If your show wants this type of exhibit, simply select the number of sprigs called for (usually ten to twenty) and be sure that they are uniform in every respect. Each sprig must be the same length and a good one is anywhere from six to ten inches. You will probably have to harvest many times the number of specimens than you need in order to select a uniform lot, but after you have selected the desired number, tie the bases of the stem together with clean, neat string or a rubber band and place the base of the bunch either in moist tissue paper or in a jar, depending on what the show requires.

This is done to avoid wilting. Actually, I like to see shows require parsley exhibited in little jars, for the specimens stay fresh for the entire show when exhibited this way.

Cole Crops BROCCOLI An exhibitable head of broccoli must be at the right stage of maturity for eating, meaning that the flowers have to be tightly budded and not expended. Wilted specimens are considered very bad, and for this reason keep the stem in water until you are ready to exhibit the specimen. Size is not the all-important factor in broccoli classes, but the larger heads that are still tender and good for eating will be favored over small heads, all other factors being equal. You should strive for a head three inches in diameter as an average size.

A bad fault of broccoli is leaves showing in the flower cluster, so it is wise to avoid such specimens. The stem should be cut neatly, straight and tidy, leaving an over-all length of six to seven inches from the top of the head to the base of the cut stem. A few of the lower leaves can be trimmed off neatly, leaving no stubs.

BRUSSELS SPROUTS One sprout does not comprise an exhibit since the judge cannot determine from so little how good a gardener and showman you actually are. For this reason you are usually requested to exhibit a quart or sometimes ten Brussels sprouts to make a representative exhibit.

All of the members of this lot must be uniform in size, shape, and color and in top-notch condition. A good general size is one inch in diameter. And of course the rule that underlies all exhibiting is important here too—freedom of blemishes of any type.

CABBAGE Some shows set up separate classes for the various cabbage types although this is not the case unless the show is predominantly one for vegetables. These types are round, flat, pointed, red, and savoy. Often the superintendent of all vegetable classes will make this division after the exhibits are in place and before the judging begins.

Pointed heads are usually lighter in weight than the other types. Therefore, using Jersey Wakefield as a variety example, your selection of Jersey should weigh about two to three pounds. The other types should weigh about three to five pounds. The heads must be symmetrical and properly shaped for the variety in question as well as crisp and firm, except in loose-headed types like savoy. All outer leaves should be removed, leaving only the last few that curl at the tips (Fig. 23).

Fig. 23. Cabbage properly prepared for the show table.

Then square off the stem neatly, leaving it about one half to one inch in length. See Photograph 7.

CAULIFLOWER A good head of cauliflower must be snow white unless you have purposely grown one of the purple varieties. "Dirty" colored heads mean that the exhibitor didn't cover the head to blanch it by protecting it from the strong sunlight. Blanching is easy to do by simply tying the long leaves over the flower head as it develops.

A good average size to select for your exhibit is a four- to five-inch-diameter head. Leave four to six of the outer leaves and allow them to extend one to two inches above the head, trimming off the rest of the blade. The stem should be two inches long below the head and neatly squared off.

Root Crops Root crops have so many common basic requirements that it seems wise to discuss them generally. We must select specimens that are free from deformities, meaning that the shape must be perfect and true to the variety. Growth cracks in the specimen, rots or decays, and the presence of rootlets will not be tolerated by the judge. Only the taproot can be present.

Sunburn is common on many of our root crops. To illustrate sunburning, let's take the carrot where its shoulder turns green when exposed to the sun. This causes a bitter flavor in the carrot, or any other root crop, so it must be avoided in selecting show material.

Usually you will be required to exhibit your root crops in lots of five with the tops cut off one to two inches above the root. Sometimes schedules call for radishes with the tops present, but usually you can remove the tops on radishes one half to one inch above the root. Any dried-up stems must be taken off the specimen for good appearance.

Now that we have mentioned these matters basic to the exhibiting of all root crops all we need to mention is the size requirements for the specific plants.

BEETS One and one-half to two and one-half inch diameters are ideal for beets. You must make sure that each member of the exhibit is uniform in size as well as shape and color. Large beets are not fit to eat nor are they fit for the show table.

CARROTS An average diameter of three-quarter inch to one and one-half inches is ideal for carrots. Each carrot in the lot must be the same size. The ox-heart types should be three to four inches long, the half-long types five to seven inches long, and the long types up to eight inches in length. See Photograph 7.

PARSNIPS The size requirements for parsnips are the same as for carrots except for length. Generally speaking, parsnips must be from five to seven inches long. Avoid the selection of hollow-crowned parsnips since they are not considered good exhibition material.

RADISHES Depending upon the variety, radishes can range from three-quarter inch to one and one-quarter inches in diameter.

TURNIPS AND RUTABAGAS Turnips should be one and one-half inches in diameter to three inches; rutabagas can range from three to four inches in diameter.

Bulb Crops ONIONS Onions must be at least two inches in diameter for show purposes. Their tops should be cut off, leaving only one to two inches on the bulb. This operation is best performed two weeks before the show when the onion is dug so that the tops have some time to dry slightly. Onions should be dried in a spot out of direct sunlight and in good air circulation. It is best to remove the rootlets of the onion when it is to be shown. Actually the rootlets do not tell very much about the culture of the onion that the bulb itself doesn't tell; therefore, leaving the rootlets on the specimen merely detracts from its over-all appearance.

Only the very outer scale can be removed from the bulb. This scale is usually cracked and dirty and its removal is necessary. However, this operation is one that requires utmost care and patience. If the showman is in a hurry and tears off this scale he may accidentally tear off part of the inner scale and then the judge's comment will be that points were deducted because the specimen was "peeled too much." So you see how very important it is to use care and exercise patience when grooming onions for the show.

Cracked scales and sunburned spots are the most common faults in onion exhibits. Aside from these factors the selection of five onions to compose a lot is relatively easy as vegetable selection goes.

Legumes BEANS Depending on the size and importance of the vegetable exhibit, many of the shows in large vegetable areas will divide the bean exhibit into at least three main areas. Shell beans, lima beans, and snap beans, either green or wax, are the most common classes for such a division.

Usually the show schedule asks for ten beans to a plate. Regardless of what type of bean they are, they must be uniform in size, shape, and color and must be at the proper stage for eating, whether limas, snaps, or shell. All of the specimens in a plate must be of the same variety and further they must have one-quarter to one-half inch of the stem present as illustrated in Figure 24. Snap and lima beans must not be wilted or

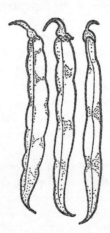

Fig. 24. Beans at the proper stage for exhibition and properly picked.

flabby. In lima beans, the bean itself must be pronounced in the pod, for this is what the crop is grown for. Snap beans, on the other hand, must only slightly show the bean in the pod, for these are not grown for the actual bean. And shell beans, of course, must clearly show the well-developed bean.

All beans, regardless of type or variety, must be straight and free from twisted and contorted parts of the pod. In some varieties it is the tendency of the pods to be curved, and when you grow this variety make sure that all ten members composing a plate are curved the same way; in other words, they must be uniform in shape.

PEAS Since peas too are in pods, the same basic points underlie their selection for the show. Usually they are exhibited as a plate of ten specimens but in some instances the schedule asks for shelled peas. This, however, is the exception rather than the rule.

Except for edible pod peas, the peas in all pods that are exhibited should be well developed and the pod must be well filled out. Often in edible pod peas, if we wait until this point, the pods are too tough, so we must exhibit them with the peas slightly developed.

All pods making up an exhibit plate must be uniform in every respect. Furthermore, a short portion of the stem must be present as well as the very tip of the pod. Broken tips, in either peas or beans, cost points on the score card.

Solanaceous Fruits TOMATOES The name "solanaceous" refers to the family Solanaceae, the nightshade family, of which tomatoes, peppers and eggplants, as well as potatoes, are members. Since potatoes are not fruits, we will discuss them in a separate division.

Depending on the size of the vegetable exhibit, tomatoes are either shown in one big class or divided into ripe reds, yellows, greens, cherry, plum, or pears. For the small show, the latter divisions may be too involved and a division of only three parts may be more practical (ripe, green, and novelty types, which would include the cherry, pear, plum, and other types).

Most often five uniform specimens two to three inches in diameter comprise a good exhibit. The novelty types do not attain this size, of course. The showman should avoid unevenly colored fruits, those with touches of rot or those which have cracked skins. Ripe tomatoes can be exhibited with the stems either on or off, but green tomatoes must always have their stems on. See Photograph 10.

PEPPERS   In the larger shows peppers are usually divided into two classes—sweet or hot. I feel that even in small shows this is a logical division.

As in tomatoes, five specimens are usually the normal number for an exhibit, but I have noticed several shows recently that require only three. All of these specimens on a plate must be uniform and possess the same number of lobes on each pepper according to the type and variety shown. Sweet peppers must be mature at the time of the show and the showmen can strive for a length of three to four inches in selecting his specimens. The stems of peppers should be neatly cut off level with the shoulders of the specimen.

Common faults like discoloration of parts of the fruit, shriveling, immaturity, and skin blemishes will not be tolerated by the judge. See Photograph 7.

EGGPLANT   In most instances, one fruit makes up an exhibit; in some of the large vegetable shows two or three specimens may be required.

The specimen must be symmetrical and true to type as well as mature. The color must be uniform over the entire fruit, and no dark spots, indicating bruising, will be tolerated. Streaks through the normal purple color of the fruit are considered very bad faults.

Dirt can be removed from eggplant by gently running a damp cloth over the fruit. The word "gently" cannot be stressed enough, for if the cloth picks up a piece of grit the skin of the fruit can be badly damaged. The stem must be cut neatly about an inch or two in length and the calyxes must be present on the show specimen.

Vine Crops This division includes pumpkins, squashes, melons, and cucumbers. In comparison to many of the other crops mentioned so far, this is one of the easiest groups to exhibit.

All specimens in this group are cleaned in the same manner mentioned for eggplant and with the same precautions. All fruits must be symmetrical and true to variety with a short portion of the stem present and neatly cut. In the larger fruits, two to three inches of the stem is necessary; in the smaller items like cucumbers and small melons, only one-half inch of stem is all that is required. Of course, all show specimens must be at their peak of maturity unless the show schedules says otherwise, as it may do in the case of watermelons when a show is early.

SUMMER SQUASH Often summer squash of all types is sown in one class, while in other cases this group is divided into crooknecks, scallops, and Italian squash (cocozelle, zucchini, and caserta).

Crooknecks and straightnecks can range from six to eight inches in length and their color must be a clear, almost lemon yellow. A hard orange yellow indicates overmaturity. The scallop types can range from three to six inches in diameter, but the Italian types must fall between eight to twelve inches in length. Two to three specimens make an exhibit. See Photograph 8.

WINTER SQUASH Hubbard and delicious squash, table queen, and butternut are likely divisions for this group. Except for the table queen and possibly butternut, entrees in this group are usually single specimens. Table queen is sometimes asked for in groups of twos.

The size range that the showman must select for is ten to eighteen inches for Hubbards, five to seven inches for the table queen types, and ten to twelve inches for butternuts. The characteristic shape for Hubbard squash is the typical protruding stem and blossom ends with a large plump central portion. An acorn shape is ideal for the table queen types, and the butternut must be of the rounded blossom end with a broad, plump stem end almost as broad as the basal rounded portion. Slim stem ends are not considered correct for butternut squash.

PUMPKINS   Symmetry, good color, maturity, and trueness to type are the characteristics the showman must exhibit in his pumpkins, regardless of variety. The size of the specimen will vary according to the variety and the showman must not feel compelled to exhibit only the largest specimen without regard to the other important requirements. Size is a popular misconception when it comes to pumpkins because over the years many fairs and shows have had classes for the largest specimen. Many shows today have such classes and while it is true that for this class, if you want to win, you must have the largest specimen it is not true for a regular garden class of pumpkins. See Photograph 8.

Melons   MUSKMELONS   All show schedules should be divided to include separate classes for watermelons and muskmelons. It is difficult for the judge to judge a class where the two types are combined.

In muskmelons usually a single specimen is required. The melon must be mature and the varieties which have netted rinds must show a clear, neat pattern of this netting. Muskmelons are the only members of this large group of vine crops on which the stem must not be present. The best way to tell whether or not a muskmelon is mature is when the stem slips off naturally. Although the melon must be mature and at the proper eating stage, it must not be overmature to the point where yellowed spots show on the rind. The stem end must be calloused and sunken on most varieties. See Photographs 9 and 11.

WATERMELONS   Symmetry in shape, good shiny color, and freedom from injury and disease are a few of the important factors to consider when selecting a watermelon for exhibition. Of course maturity is of utmost importance too and this is perhaps more difficult to determine in watermelons than in muskmelons. Usually, if the white spot that develops where the melon touches the ground has turned yellow, you can be fairly sure that your melon is mature. Although this is not a foolproof test, it works in a high percentage of cases. The judge does have the privilege of removing a core of rind and meat from the melon with his knife if there is any question in his mind as to the melon's maturity.

In watermelons it is important to leave from a half to a full inch of stem. When the stem is torn off in picking the fruit it leaves a wonderful scar for the evaporation of water which in turn deteriorates the quality of the melon.

CUCUMBERS   This vegetable is often listed in two categories on show schedules—slicing and pickling. From three to five specimens are required in most slicing classes; five to ten specimens are asked for in pickling classes.

Cucumbers must possess a good, symmetrical shape which is true to variety. Misshapen fruits indicate, as a general rule, poor culture. The color should be a good green and the fruit must be at the proper stage of maturity for its intended purpose. One-half inch of stem must be present.

Gourds   While gourds are not edible vegetables, I list them, here, for they are not flowers either. It seems to me that for the sake of clarity they fit best into this category of vine crops.

Usually show schedules call for a collection of five gourds, but in some instances the number is increased, depending on the desires and intent of the show committee. Unless the show schedule reads "five gourds, one variety," it is all right to assume that mixed types and varieties are acceptable in the lot of five.

If gourds have a definite color pattern, it must be clear and distinct. Indistinct color patterns indicate that the specimen or specimens are not true to type. In other respects, the same basic rules for exhibiting summer squash are followed in the exhibition of gourds.

Corn There are many points to keep foremost in the exhibition of this crop. In addition to the basic pointers for all vegetables and flowers, we must be sure to follow others peculiar to this plant.

Corn classes are often divided into sweet corn and popcorn. This division is a just one and every show should have it. Most of the corn exhibited at shows is sweet corn. The schedules usually call for from three to five ears to a plate, or exhibit, and these must be uniform in every respect. The stem of the ear must be neatly cut off just below the point where the husks are attached to it. If this cut is made too high, the husks will fall off and ruin the over-all appearance of the specimen.

Although judges vary in the next point, most will agree that the silk should be removed from the ear before the ear is placed on the show table. This makes the judging job easier for the judge, and the show committee is appreciative since the table is not littered with silk after the judging is over. While removing the silk, by turning back the husks as one would in normal removal, you are given the opportunity to see whether the ears are filled out all the way to the tip and also whether earworms are present. Every ear should be filled out completely with kernels if good scoring results are expected, and the lines or rows of kernels should be straight except in those varieties where crooked rows are typical. Judges hate to open the husks and see a worm wiggling about. So when you remove the silk, you also accomplish these inspections; after doing so, neatly turn the husks back as they originally were. Never exhibit husked corn.

Although we have already mentioned that proper maturity is important in every crop, it is so easy to go wrong with corn that we will mention it again. In selecting corn for the show table, you will probably have to pick many more ears than you will exhibit. On some of the ears that are not exhibitable, but come from the same planting as those that are, try the finger test for maturity. Press your finger into a kernel. If the juice that comes out is sluggish and syrupy, then the ear is over-mature. If the juice is light and milky and really squirts out of the kernel, then you have selected an ear that is proper. I suggest again that you do this on specimens that you will not exhibit, for if you do it on the show specimens the judge will consider them injured.

Lastly, see that the color of the kernels is not only uniform within the ear but within the entire lot of ears that you exhibit.

Potatoes IRISH POTATOES Potatoes, like the other crops, must be uniform in size, shape, and color; this usually means that you will have to dig many more than you need for the exhibit in order to find a uniform five. The digging should be done a week or two prior to the show so that they will have time to dry a little.

Potatoes should be an average of from two and one-quarter to four inches in length and the larger ones should not weigh more than sixteen ounces. The smaller ones must meet a minimum weight requirement of six ounces.

Be sure that the potatoes you exhibit are mature, cured slightly, and free of soil. Dirty potatoes will be disqualified as will scrubbed potatoes. Wash them with a soft cloth. See Photograph 7.

SWEET POTATOES Like Irish potatoes, sweet potatoes must be

clean, free from disease and dirt, and uniform in every respect. They too must be dug at least a week before the show so that they will have an opportunity to cure slightly.

Different varieties of sweet potatoes differ in shape. Some are spindle shaped, while others are globular. Either shape is permissible depending on the variety, but its shape must be uniform throughout the plate of five. Each specimen must weigh between one-half to one pound and this weight must be uniform throughout the exhibit. An average diameter of between two to three inches is best and a length of two to three times the diameter is ideal.

Fruit   The basic factors that underlie the selection of flowers and vegetables also govern the selection of fruits. We have discussed these factors so many times that it would be boring and repetitious to do it again here.

Most fruit judges use the following score card or a slight variation of it in judging fruit.

Condition, including freedom from blemishes	30 points
Uniformity of size, shape, and color	25 points
Color	20 points
Size	15 points
Form	10 points
Total	100 points

I am sure that the first two points in this score card are clear and except for calling your attention to the number of points that these two demand on the score card any further discussion is unnecessary. The other items, however, may need some discussion here.

Color on this score card refers to the intensity for the variety in question. Color should be high in fruit as in most other horticultural specimens. But in this case, color is set off as an item demanding twenty points since in fruit it is color which gives eye-appeal and indicates a great deal as far as condition is concerned.

Size in the case of fruit refers to the ideal size of a certain variety; form refers to the characteristic shape for a said variety, depending upon the area of the country in which the specimens were grown. We cannot list any specific pointers as to these two matters since they vary in different parts of the country.

APPLES   Five apples is what the show schedule usually requires at most shows, although in some cases the show committee decides that only three are enough. The stems of all specimens must be present, but not the fruiting spur or leaves from the spur. See Photograph 12.

PEARS   Five medium-sized fruits with stems attached comprise a plate for exhibition. The color, sizes, and shape must be uniform and the specimens free from blemish or injury. Over- or undermaturity will not be tolerated by the judge unless the schedule permits it because of the time of the show. See Photograph 9.

PEACHES   Peaches, like other fruit, must be uniform in every respect with the ground color of the fruit yellow. Red cheeks will vary with varieties and will not be demanded by the judge unless it is typical of the variety.

The stems of peaches need not be present and each member of a lot must be uniform in this respect. Since it is easy to bruise a peach, the showman must take great care at the time of harvesting and during the transportation of the specimens to the show. Avoid the selection of overripe specimens for exhibition purposes.

PLUMS AND CHERRIES   Shows will vary in the number of specimens you need to exhibit in these fruits. Some require ten to a dozen specimens on a plate; others require either a pint basket or a quart basket full. In either case, do what the show schedule demands but make sure that you leave the stems attached in both crops. Select only the plump, ripe specimens and make sure that they are uniform throughout the exhibit. Bloom, the white substance on plums, must not be removed.

GRAPES From three to five bunches make an exhibit of grapes. Each bunch or cluster must be uniform in size and the fruit on the bunch must be in good condition with the bloom present. The stem of each cluster must be neatly cut and preferably the same length on each cluster. Any decayed portion of the cluster can be neatly removed, but be careful not to detach any of the good parts. Each grape must be firmly attached if good results are expected.

RASPBERRIES AND BLACKBERRIES Usually only a pint box of fruit is required with these fruits. Make sure that each specimen is uniform in size, shape, and color within the box and that uniformity of ripeness also exists. Each fruit should be clean, free of injury of mechanical origin as well as pest injury.

BLUEBERRIES Again, only a pint box is required at most shows. The berries must be uniformly plump and ripe with as much of the bloom present on the fruit as possible. The showman must be careful not to tear the fruit at picking time. Each berry must be of the same variety in each lot.

STRAWBERRIES Either pint or quart boxes of strawberries may be required, depending upon the show. Each berry within the box must be uniform in size, shape, and color, and each berry must also have the stem and "cap" attached. Green-streaked berries or malformed members are common faults with this crop and should be avoided. Also, be certain to clean the specimens before placing them on the show table. As mentioned earlier, dirt can be removed with a soft painter's brush. Strawberries must never be washed prior to a show.

PART THREE

Grooming

10

Conditioning and Grooming

After we are through judging horticultural material at a fair, my wife and I just delight in walking through the livestock tents. It is almost unbelievable to see the amount of work that goes into the grooming of livestock. The herdsman spends many hours brushing the animal's coat to eliminate loose hairs and to make it shine. The tail of the animal is first washed, sometimes bleached, and then braided while it is still wet so that it will be curly and fluffy when finally brushed out. Before the cattle even come to the fair their hoofs are trimmed and shaped and sanded down to make them clean and shiny. Then the horns are first sanded with regular paper and then finally gone over with emery cloth and mineral oil so that they will enhance the appearance of the animal.

These are only a few of the grooming techniques that I know about and I am sure that there are many more that go on when I am not around. When we see how thoroughly the livestock is groomed, we can't help thinking of a few of the specimens that we judged, such as those with dirty lower leaves or those with spray residue present.

The grooming of horticultural specimens for a show is not

nearly so much work as the grooming of an animal; nevertheless, it does take some time and patience. It is, though, the best time that you will ever devote to the long process of producing a specimen for the show, for good grooming is what makes an exhibit. No grooming at all can literally ruin an otherwise perfect blue ribbon entry.

PICKING AND CONDITIONING

Conditioning means to properly treat a specimen so that it will stand up well after it reaches the show. Good conditioning begins the moment the stem of a flower, fruit, or vegetable is severed from the parent plant in the garden. A good sharp knife is one of the many factors that contribute to proper conditioning. When a dull knife is used, it is possible to constrict the water-conducting vessels of the specimen when the cut is made, thus shortening its life span. Shears, if sharp, are the second best tool for cutting stems, but since you have two blades coming together in their cutting action, you risk the chance of some constriction here also. Hence, we say that a good, sharp knife is the best cutting tool.

The showman must carry with him in the garden a pail of warm water in which to place the stems of flowers. Technically, this water should be at a temperature of 110 degrees, or the temperature of bath water, realizing that people prefer different bath temperatures. It is best to draw the water five to ten minutes before going into the garden so that most of the air bubbles dissolve. More than three to four inches of water in the pail are unnecessary.

It is believed that warm water moves more freely into the stem of flowers. Some researchers theorize that warm water also dissolves any air bubbles in the conducting vessels of the stem more quickly than cold water.

If the warm water treatment is to be of any use, the flower stem must be placed into it immediately after it is cut. For this reason, the low, sideless basket sold in many garden shops especially for the collecting of cut flowers in the garden is of no use when show specimens are being collected. Many of the flowers that produce milky or sticky sap, however, condition best if they are placed in cold water. The Nehrlings in their book *Gardening, Forcing, and Conditioning for Flower Arrangements* tell us that daffodils, dahlias, poinsettias, fuschias, forget-me-nots, and poppies require cold water for conditioning rather than warm water. This group, then, is the exception to the warm water conditioning rule.

You have probably noticed that many of our garden flowers exude their sap when they are cut from the plant. Therefore, their stems must be seared to "seal up" the sap and prevent too much of it from being lost. Hollyhocks, poppies, dahlias, daffodils, poinsettias, heliotrope, plume poppy, milkweed, and cardinal flower are members of the group that requires searing. This step can be accomplished very easily by placing the freshly cut stem in boiling water for one minute or in a flame for one-half minute before placing the flower in the conditioning pail.

Many showmen stress the importance of cutting the stems of flowers on a slant "so that they will take in more water." This belief is erroneous because the slanted cut does not appreciably increase the conducting tissue. Post states in his book *Florist Crop Production and Marketing* that the prime benefit of cutting a stem on a slant is that these stems do not squarely touch the bottom of a container when placed in it and for this reason the conducting vessels are less likely to become clogged up with dirt. He further states that stems cut more easily on a slant than square across.

It has been found beneficial, however, to crush the lower two inches of woody stems with a blunt object before conditioning them. These types of stems do conduct water to some degree through the tissue between the xylem tubes as well as through the tubes themselves. The main difference between woody and non-woody stems is that the former have more tissue between the xylem tubes than the latter. Chrysanthemums, phlox, lythrum, stock, and the woody shrubs are among the plants that benefit from stem crushing.

We have strayed a bit from the matter of picking flowers from the garden to discuss some exceptions to the general rules. In conclusion, then, we can say that most flowers should be placed in warm water as soon after picking as possible. The container holding the flowers should then be placed at cool temperatures, specifically 40 to 45 degrees. For most showmen, unless they have a refrigerator specifically for the purpose, the best place to condition flowers is on a cool basement floor. The spot selected should be dark and out of drafts and the flowers should be left in this location for at least twelve hours previous to the show. It is easy to see that we are trying to find conditions that do not favor water loss or a high respiration rate.

Usually the original amount of water that you placed in the pail will be enough for the entire conditioning process, but in some cases, such as with the woody material, more water may be necessary before the process is completed. In this case, cold water can be added since the water in the conditioning pail is already cold. If for some reason a few of the flowers have wilted, simply remove them from the pail, re-cut the stem, place them in warm water, and they will probably come back to life. In other words, you are repeating the whole process in an effort to revive the wilted specimen.

The humidity in the conditioning process should be as high as possible. Some authorities recommend syringing the foliage of the flowers, but this can be dangerous because the blossoms of many flowers will spot badly when droplets of water fall on them. Delphiniums, dahlias, lupines, petunias, and roses are but a few of those that will spot. Furthermore, free water on any portion of the plant encourages disease invasion if temperature conditions are favorable. If you do syringe your specimens, do it sparingly, but better yet, place a plastic bag over the entire pail and its contents in an effort to raise the humidity by trapping the moisture which is evaporating from the base of the pail or transpiring through the foliage.

Specimens that are being conditioned cannot be crowded without risking the possibility of some injury to the foliage, stem, or blossoms. Even non-crowded flowers that rub against the side of the pail can be damaged. For this reason it is wise to devise some means of holding flowers erect and in an uncrowded condition. To accomplish this, some showmen place shredded stryoform in the base of the pail; others prefer to construct a wire mesh frame (Fig. 25). One of the frames is

Fig. 25. A wire mesh holding rack.

placed within two inches of the bottom of the pail, while the other can be adjusted at the proper height for the material in question. For example, leafless scapes of hemerocallis cause little concern, but stems of phlox or marigolds, which have leaves, may necessitate placing the two mesh frames closer together. The showman must remember, however, that when the specimens are finally placed on the show table the lower foliage which will be under water must be removed anyway. Therefore, it could be removed at conditioning time so that the wire mesh frames could be used to hold the flowers erect and straight.

The question always arises as to whether or not to use conditioners in the conditioning process. Showmen have different opinions on this subject but my answer is that the process is so short that we can save time by beginning their use when the flowers are placed on the show table.

There are many good conditioners on the market which are designed to do two things. First, they should lower the pH of the water to discourage bacterial growth; second, they add carbohydrates to the water and eventually to the flowers so that that which is lost through respiration will be replaced at least in part.

Many experiment stations have found that the addition of a tablespoon of white vinegar and two tablespoons of sugar to a quart of water makes an excellent conditioner. I have found this mixture to be especially good for roses because it prevents petal drop from the specimen. Usually petal drop is not a problem for one or two day shows, but for longer events it definitely is.

So far our discussion of picking and conditioning has dealt primarily with flowers. In the case of vegetables, it is better to pick and prepare them just before the show if you have time. This is also true of fruit. In Chapter 9 we mentioned a few exceptions to this general statement.

When flowers and vegetables come into prime exhibiting condition a few days before the show, it is then wise to pick them and place them at 40- to 45-degree temperatures. This type of produce does not take up too much room and for this reason the kitchen refrigerator can be used for short periods. Sometimes when vegetables are stored in the refrigerator and removed to warm show temperatures the skin tends to shrivel, especially on tomatoes. For this reason, remove the vegetables from the refrigerator a few hours before the show and place them in a cool spot, but one slightly warmer than the refrigerator. In this way you gradually raise the temperature and the vegetable becomes acclimated to its future temperature less abruptly.

It is easy to injure the surface of fruits or vegetables at picking time. Extreme care should be used in handling this produce; it should be placed in a cloth or paper-lined basket with pieces of paper between each specimen. This cuts down on mechanical injury greatly and ensures good appearance. It doesn't pay to pack too many vegetables or fruits in one basket, for the weight of one upon another can cause bruising. This is especially true in the case of soft material such as tomatoes, peppers, and berries.

A good sharp knife or shears must be used in the picking of most vegetables or fruit. In Chapter 9 we mentioned that beans, peas, eggplants, peppers, strawberries, and many others should be exhibited with part of the stem attached. If we try to pick this material without a knife or shears, it is highly possible that this stem will break off.

GROOMING

The matter of grooming show specimens is the last step in the growing for showing process before transporting the material to the show. Although some accounts on grooming mention disbudding, we have stressed that this operation must be done while the specimen is growing in the garden. Actually all we have to do at this point is to remove any soil or dirt that is on the foliage, stem, or flower and also remove all spray residue. In the case of house plants, the pot must be thoroughly cleaned, spray residue removed, and any leaves that have yellowed in the few days previous to the show should be removed. Flowers that have passed their prime must also be removed from house plants during this process.

The removal of soil from a flower or plant is a relatively simple matter; the only hard thing about the process is the patience which it demands. If we are in a hurry, it is possible to damage the foliage by either breaking it or by grinding soil into it and thus injuring its tissue. For this reason, give yourself plenty of time for this step. Any loose soil can be removed by a slight force of water from either a faucet or a syringe. The remaining finer particles will come off under running water with the aid of a soft flannel cloth. If soil particles, or in some cases soot or dust, persist, syringe the foliage with mild soapy water; then loosen the particles with a soft cloth and wash them off with a gentle water force.

Not only must you allow plenty of time for this process, but you must also do it well in advance of the show. I have seen specimens on the show table that were washed, but on which all of the dirt did not come off. The foliage in this case was streaked and a second washing was necessary. Unfortunately the just judge has to admit that you tried, but he still has to mark your specimen down.

Spray residue is removed in exactly the same manner, but here your patience is tried to a greater degree because some residues are reluctant to come off. I find that syringing the plant with a soapy water, gently rubbing it with a soft cloth, and then applying a gentle force of water works very well. Dr. Cynthia Wescott, in her article on insect and disease control in *The Handbook of Flower Shows* published by the National Council of State Garden Clubs, suggests that spray residues can be removed by rubbing the foliage with a piece of soft cotton or nylon stocking. This is an effective way to remove residues, especially when their presence is not too severe.

We need not say more about the trimming of fruits and vegetables since this was discussed in the last chapter. The cleaning of them, however, is a problem that should concern us here. It saddens me to think of all of the plates of vegetables that I have had to score down because they were scrubbed too much. Vegetables or fruits must not be scrubbed with a brush because the bristles gash the surface and leave them unattractive and vulnerable to high water loss through the gashes. It seems logical to scrub vegetables since this is what we do before cooking them. But here they go immediately into the pot and do not have to be judged or sit for at least a day on a show table to be viewed by all.

Fruits and vegetables should be washed with a soft cloth after first removing as much of the loose soil as possible under a faucet or hose nozzle. The root crop will need several washings so that they will not streak. At this time any dried leaf petioles on carrots or beets can be removed. Strawberries and other soft fruits cannot be rubbed even with a soft cloth, so here we have to rely entirely upon a gentle flow of water.

Before leaving the subject of grooming we need to say a word or two about the application of materials to the foliage of house plants to make it shine. This practice is not considered proper in the exhibition of plant material. In fact, the judge will severely score down your points if these "leaf shining" materials are used. I, for one, disqualify the plant entirely, regardless of its other points. Leaves can be made to shine by rubbing them with a dry flannel cloth. This practice brings out the natural oils in the leaf, making it appear just as lovely as, and I think more lovely than, through artificial means.

TRANSPORTATION TO THE SHOW

Just one little slip in the manner in which you transport your entries to the show can ruin all of your growing and grooming efforts. I personally feel that here is where most of the mechanical injury found on show specimens occurs. I hate to think of all of the specimens that I have had to grade down in my short judging career just because of mechanical injury. The showman has to put considerable time and effort into growing show material; he might just as well devote a few extra minutes to proper carrying techniques for his entries. This time will be well spent.

It would be well worth your while to construct a carrying rack in which to place your specimens for transporting. There are many types of racks that you can make right at home with very little expense and effort. The wire mesh frames which we discussed in relation to conditioning are one type of rack that can be used. Simply leave the flowers in the conditioning pail and carry them to the show.

Tin cans make excellent carrying racks if mounted on a base board. As you know, there are many sizes of cans ranging from the small frozen juice concentrate size to the large liquid juice size; in addition, there are even larger cans which restaurants discard. The very small juice cans are excellent for small materials like violets, pansies, and alyssum. The medium-sized cans such as those used for canned vegetables and fruit are suitable for material like ageratum, petunias, and dwarf marigolds, while the large cans are best for the larger flowers.

It is wise to make the rack in the winter when you have more time. To make the base, obtain a pine board ten to twelve inches wide and three feet long. In order to determine the right spacings for the cans on the board, lay them out and trace, with a pencil, around their bases. Allow at least three to four inches between the small cans and six to eight inches between the larger ones. Then with a drill bore a one-half-inch hole to the side of each can and place a dowel in it. Permit the dowel to be six inches above the height of each can so the specimen can be tied to it for the trip to the show. This keeps the specimen from rolling and rubbing around and becoming damaged. You may want to extend the dowel one foot to eighteen inches above the can in cases where you will be carrying tall material such as iris and gladioli.

With a fine-gauged wire, such as that used for corsage making or picture hanging, tightly fasten the can to the dowel in two places. Three brads can be driven into the base board around each can to keep the cans from sliding around. Lastly, paint the rack for appearance and long life (Fig. 26).

The advantage of a rack of this type is that it is easy to make; the only tools needed are a drill, hammer, pliers, and a paint brush. The cans can be changed from show to show to fit the size of material being transported. Also, it is inexpensive to build and can be used for conditioning as well.

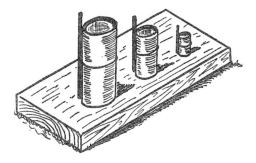

Fig. 26. The tin can carrying rack.

Some showmen may want to build a handle on the rack for extra ease.

Even though the tin can rack is easy to build, it may involve too much work for the gardener who exhibits only occasionally. This person could devise a satisfactory case by placing waxed cartons, such as those used for milk, cream, and juice, in a box and separating them with newspapers. The cone-shaped cartons are especially good since very little tipping occurs with them.

House plants, too, should be carried in a box with newspapers stuffed between each pot, allowing plenty of room for the plant itself. Even if you have just one plant, place it in a box with newspapers stuffed between the pot and the sides of the box. This procedure makes a base for the pot so that it will not tip over.

Some showmen advocate the carrying of large material such as dahlias and gladioli in a long florist's box out of water. It is my opinion, however, that all material should be carried in water. The fewer times we remove the specimens from water, the better their chance for remaining in good condition. Therefore, a carrying case of some type should be used, be it a pail, a tin can rack, or another device you care to invent.

To avoid any possible damage to the tender petals of your flowers, invest in a package or two of tissue paper for wrapping the blooms. This is purely a safety step that often pays dividends. Simply use a large piece of paper, place it over the bloom loosely, and wrap it around the base of the flower or flower head, being careful not to crowd the florets or petals (Fig. 27).

Fig. 27. A flower covered with tissue paper for protection.

All vegetables and fruits must be wrapped in either tissue paper or newspaper to prevent bruising. With small vegetables, such as ten pea pods selected for a plate exhibit, you can wrap them all together in one piece of paper. The wrapped produce can be packed in a shallow box with newspapers stuffed between each package as cushioning. The use of a low, shallow box is important, for the packing of produce in a deep box causes too much weight and injury on the bottom ones. Soft material, like strawberries and tomatoes, must be packaged separately.

Playful children or pets are best left at home for the trip to the show. A foot of either in a box of tomatoes or house plants could be disastrous. Most children, however, if included in the whole growing for showing procedure, will have just as much pride in and respect for the finished product to be exhibited as you. Include them if you can to develop future showmen and gardeners!

So goes the interesting art and science of growing for showing. Time, devotion, and patience are the bywords of this rewarding and satisfying experience.

Index

A

African violets, 78, 80
Ageratum, 92, 93
All-purpose sprays and dusts, 74
Altering flowers, 69
Ammonium nitrate, 38
Apples, 121
Asparagus, 104
Aster, 93
Availability, nutrients, 28, 29

B

Beans, 112, 113
Beets, 110
Blueberries, 122
Broccoli, 108
Brussel sprouts, 108

C

Cabbage, 108
Calcium, 24, 25
Calendula, 92
Captan, 74
Carrots, 110
Cauliflower, 109

Celery, 106, 107
Chard, 105
Chelated iron, 31
Cherries, 121, 122
Chlorosis, 23, 24; iron, 30, 31
Chrysanthemums, 42–44, 94
Cleaning: vegetables and fruit, 103, 104
Cockscomb, 87
Coleus. See potted plants
Color, 82, 102, 120
Conditioning, 50; thirty-one degree storage, 50–54; definition, 126; method, 126–31; storage, 130–31
Containers. See potted plants
Corn, 118–19
Cucumbers, 117
Cultural perfection, 85, 86, 103

D

Daffodils, 98
Dahlia, 95–96
Damage: freedom of, 84; mechanical, 84; pests, 84–85; spray, 85; weather, 85